The Lake District
A DOG WALKER'S GUIDE

Peter Naldrett

COUNTRYSIDE BOOKS
NEWBURY BERKSHIRE

First published 2014
© Peter Naldrett 2014
Reprinted 2018, 2023

All rights reserved. No reproduction
permitted without the prior permission
of the publisher:

COUNTRYSIDE BOOKS
3 Catherine Road
Newbury, Berkshire

To view our complete range of books,
please visit us at
www.countrysidebooks.co.uk

ISBN 978 1 84674 321 4

Photography by the author and Joe Cornish (p26); The Forestry Commission (pp1, 44, 48, 57, 58, 75); Neil Holt (pp92, 95); Jason Kaye (pp12, 38, 63, 83); The National Trust (p69); Barry Paley (pp14, 41); Jean Patefield (pp9, 22, 36, 45, 54, 76, 80, 88); Helen Reynolds (p84); and Peter Rydall (pp18, 29).

All materials used in the production of this book carry FSC certification.

Designed by Peter Davies, Nautilus Design
Produced through The Letterworks Ltd., Reading
Typeset by KT Designs, St Helens
Printed by The Holywell Press, Oxford

Contents

Introduction 5
🐾 Advice for Dog Walkers 7

Walk

1 Dodd Fell *(2.7 miles)* 9
2 Keswick – A Railway Walk *(7 miles)* 14
3 Buttermere *(2.9 miles)* 18
4 Whinlatter *(1.6 miles)* 22
5 Ennerdale Water *(7.3 miles)* 26
6 Cleator Moor *(2.3 miles)* 31
7 The Bowder Stone *(1.1 miles)* 36
8 Patterdale *(7 miles)* 41
9 Thirlmere *(1.8 miles)* 45
10 Kentmere *(6 miles)* 49
11 South Grizedale *(2.5 miles)* 54
12 Grizedale Tarn *(3.5 miles)* 58
13 Elterwater *(2.7 miles)* 63
14 Tarn Hows *(2 miles)* 67
15 Tilberthwaite *(3 miles)* 71
16 Rydal Water *(2.6 miles)* 76
17 Sizergh *(2.8 miles)* 80
18 Wray Castle *(2.7 miles)* 84
19 Kendal *(4 miles)* 88
20 Eskdale *(8.5 miles)* 92

Appendix

🐾 Contact details for small animal veterinary practices in the Lake District 96

Area map showing location of the walks.

INTRODUCTION

For me, there's nowhere in the country like the Lake District. There's not another region that keeps pulling me back, surprising me with every visit and opening up more exciting places to explore every time I go. The beauty of the Lakes lies not only in the stretches of water, but in the mountain tops, the rolling lower fells, the forests, and the views from the peaks. It's not just the natural features that make it so appealing, either. The fact that there are so many warm and welcoming pubs to choose from after a day's hiking is important too.

For dog walkers exploring this beautiful landscape, there's research to be done to make sure that the day's walking will be suitable for you both. The fells are classic sheep-farming territory and virtually every recommended stroll in the popular guide books will feature an encounter with the local Herdwick variety. There are also stiles to climb over, rocky sections of paths, steep sections, areas where the law says dogs must be on leads, and country roads that can be a danger.

I've spent many months researching this book and here you'll find some of the most accessible and suitable dog walks in the Lake District. I've spoken with local dog owners to find out their favourite routes, checked the recommendations on the Internet and talked to all the Tourist Information Centres to pinpoint the best spots. Then I've spent many weeks in the Lake District doing the walks for myself and confirming that they are suitable. None of these walks are too energetic; I've tried to keep them on the shorter side to make them accessible to all rather than being a tough slog for you and your pet. But, if you do want to challenge yourself a bit further, there are some walks where I have suggested ways you could extend your Lakeland adventure.

The walks avoid areas where there are stiles, and they are designed to keep away from livestock as much as possible. But please keep in mind that this is the Lake District and the reason why it is so popular with walkers is because it is rural, remote, rugged farming country. It is, then, pretty much impossible to head off on walks in the most scenic corners of the National Park without coming across sheep and the odd cow. The walks in this book include as much off-lead time as possible, but use common sense as to when you do have to use one.

As well as focusing on the walks, I've tried to make this much more than a book that simply directs you along countryside paths. What you have in your hand, I hope you'll agree, is more of a complete guide to these areas. I've spent time researching the towns and villages you'll visit and included information about things to do and the rich history of Lake District settlements. After all, it's much more interesting to wander through the countryside if you know a little bit about the places you are travelling through. And, most

The Lake District – A Dog Walker's Guide

importantly for some, there are pubs! Each walk recommends local dog-friendly pubs where you can rest after the walk, get some ale and a good meal.

The book has been a lot of fun to put together. I've covered classic walks where you'll see dozens of people and also more secret affairs where you may be one of only a handful out taking a stroll. If you and your dog enjoy these walks as much as I have, then you're in for a fantastic time in Cumbria.

Peter Naldrett
www.peter-naldrett.co.uk

Acknowledgements

I would like to thank Nicola, Toby, Willow, Neil, James and Rune for joining me on the walks. I am also extremely grateful to Neil Holt and the Forestry Commission for supplying some of the photographs, as well as to Heather from the wonderful National Trust for allowing me to use some images.

....

PUBLISHER'S NOTE

We hope that you obtain considerable enjoyment from this book; great care has been taken in its preparation. Although at the time of publication all routes followed public rights of way or permitted paths, diversion orders can be made and permissions withdrawn.

We cannot, of course, be held responsible for such diversion orders and any inaccuracies in the text which result from these or any other changes to the routes nor any damage which might result from walkers trespassing on private property. We are anxious though that all details covering the walks are kept up to date and would therefore welcome information from readers which would be relevant to future editions.

The simple sketch maps that accompany the walks in this book are based on notes made by the author whilst checking out the routes on the ground. They are designed to show you how to reach the start, to point out the main features of the overall circuit and they contain a progression of numbers that relate to the paragraphs of the text.

However, for the benefit of a proper map, we do recommend that you purchase the relevant Ordnance Survey sheet covering your walk. The Ordnance Survey maps are widely available, especially through booksellers and local newsagents.

ADVICE FOR DOG WALKERS

There's nothing more liberating, exciting or exhilarating than heading out into the Lake District countryside for a walk with your dog. The excursions recommended in this book can be even more enjoyable, both for you and other people, if you follow some simple guidelines to protect the countryside, its wildlife and those who enjoy it.

1 Clean it up
Nobody likes seeing dog mess at the side of paths, and certainly nobody likes to step in it or see their children step in it then trail it back to the car. There are bags available at a wide range of places so please pick it up and put it in a bin. There is nothing that can spoil a walk more than stepping in dog mess, or seeing plastic bags full of dog mess thrown into nearby bushes, left hanging on trees or stuffed into walls.

2 Watch out for other people
Be aware of other people who are using the path you are on. If there are runners, cyclists or horse riders they could very easily startle your dog, or your dog could startle them. Put your dog on a lead in busy areas where there are many bikes or horses. Be aware also that some people might not want to be approached by your dog, especially if they have young children.

3 Take a lead and be ready to use it
If you are walking on a public path in the Lake District you do not have to put your dog on a lead, the one exception to this being when you are in Copeland Borough. However, your dog must always be under control. Be aware that your dog will come across a wide range of different scents and noises. So keep your pet close to you at all times and, if you can't rely on obedience, it's best to use a lead. Note also that if you are on Access Land (and there's lots of it in these walks) you must keep your dog on a short, fixed lead no more than two metres long between lambing and nesting time, starting on 1st March and ending on 31st July.

4 Consider local wildlife
Disturbance of ground-based nests during the breeding season can lead to eggs failing to hatch. Dogs may also scare adult birds away from their nests, leaving the chicks unguarded and open to attack from predators, so keep your dog on a lead during nesting time. You should also observe local signs which can provide more up-to-date information and advice.

The Lake District – A Dog Walker's Guide

5 Be careful when heading through farms
Farmers will naturally be defensive of their livestock as they are their business and way of life. The bottom line is that if your dog starts troubling and worrying the livestock, then the farmer is allowed to get out his gun and shoot it. Completing the walks in this book, I have seen a few signs threatening as much, and warning people to have full control of their dogs on farmland. Even if your dog is friendly and normally well behaved, the sheep could still perceive it as a threat and, were they to become distressed, it could lead to young animals being killed. Cows are a different story; it is possible they could become curious about you and sometimes aggressive. If they do approach you, they may be interested in protecting their young, so don't take any chances. Drop the dog's lead and focus on getting yourself to a place of safety; your dog will be able to get clear of any danger without you. Keeping your dog on a lead when heading close to farmyards will help to avoid any difficult situations with farmers and their animals.

6 Ticks and adders
Ticks can potentially carry harmful diseases. They look like small, dark, smooth peas on the skin, and it's possible your dog could encounter them in the Lake District. Check for them regularly, and if you suspect your dog has ticks do not squeeze or pull them out. Instead, give your vet a call and ask their advice. For insect stings, scrape it away using either a finger nail or a credit card. Cool the area with a wet cloth as this may help to reduce the pain, but if you're in any doubt then call a vet. You are unlikely to encounter adders, but if you think your dog has been bitten by one, try not to let it walk any further and, if possible, carry it to the car and go to see a vet, leaving the bite wound alone.

7 Take care in the heat
It may be wishful thinking, but it is possible that you'll be in the Lake District during a spell of sunny weather. If this is the case, keep in mind that there are some strenuous paths and steep slopes in the National Park. This could lead your dog to over-exert itself and there is also the possibility of heat stroke. Symptoms may include heavy panting and difficulty in normal breathing. If you suspect this, try to keep your dog calm and move into a shaded area. If possible, get into a cool room and chill your dog by putting water over their whole body, but especially the head. Call a vet and make sure there is plenty of water for your dog to drink.

8 Have fun!
This section of the book must seem like a catalogue of nightmare situations that could go wrong in the Lake District. The reality is that the vast majority of Lake District strolls with dogs are uneventful and only go towards proving what a dog-friendly place the Lakes can be.

1

Dodd Fell

Dodd Fell is part of the Skiddaw mountain range.

This hearty stroll gives you the chance to top one of Wainwright's legendary 214 fells, all the time enjoying the woodland atmosphere and some outstanding views. For your dog, there are streams to splash in and woodland scents to investigate on this easily accessible mountain.

This relatively small but fairly challenging fell is one of the 214 Lakeland peaks that have come to be known as 'The Wainwrights', after being described and sketched by Alfred Wainwright in his classic series of books. The Wainwrights have become one of the most popular types of 'peak bagging' in the country, and the Long Distance Walkers Association keeps a list of the people who have stood atop every fell; some of them have even completed the challenge more than once! When you reach the top of Dodd Fell today you will have fantastic views all around, from Bassenthwaite down to Derwent Water and Keswick. But that was not always the case. Located on Forestry Commission land, the pine forest used to go right up to the summit and it wasn't until 2001 that the peak was cleared and allowed to revert to heather moorland. Alfred Wainwright had been a campaigner for this, going right back

The Lake District – A Dog Walker's Guide

to the 1960s. When you stand at the summit, you're actually 502 m above sea level; don't be worried by the spot height of 491 m on the OS map as that is for a location 100 m away from the highest point. A great place for wildlife, people come to Dodd Fell to get a view of ospreys nesting at Bassenthwaite and it's also a stronghold for red squirrels, a couple of which ran across the path while I was researching this walk.

Terrain
This is an exhilarating walk to the fell top with some steep inclines, but the paths and tracks are all easy to follow.

Where to park
The Forestry Commission car park at Dodd Fell (GR NY235281). **Map:** OS Explorer OL4 The English Lakes: North-western area.

How to get there
Leave the M6 at Junction 40 and head for Keswick on the A66. As you reach the Keswick area, take the turning off to the right signed for Carlisle and follow the A591 until you reach the car park on the right.

Nearest refreshments
There is a café in the car park at Dodd Fell, an ideal setting for a coffee and a bite to eat after the walk, with plenty of seating outside. Keswick is the nearest large settlement where a good bet, if you want a pub, is the Pheasant Inn on Crossthwaite Road. ☎ 01768 772219, CA12 5PP, www.pheasantinnkeswick.co.uk

Dog factors
Distance: 2.7 miles.
Road walking: None.
Livestock: None.
Stiles: None.
Nearest vets: Millcroft Veterinary Group, Southey Hill, Keswick.

The Walk

1 From the car park head towards the **Old Sawmill Tearoom**. From here, head up to where the series of trails start. Follow the **Dodd Summit** trail, which takes you over a bridge. After the bridge, turn left on the track that takes you

Dodd Fell

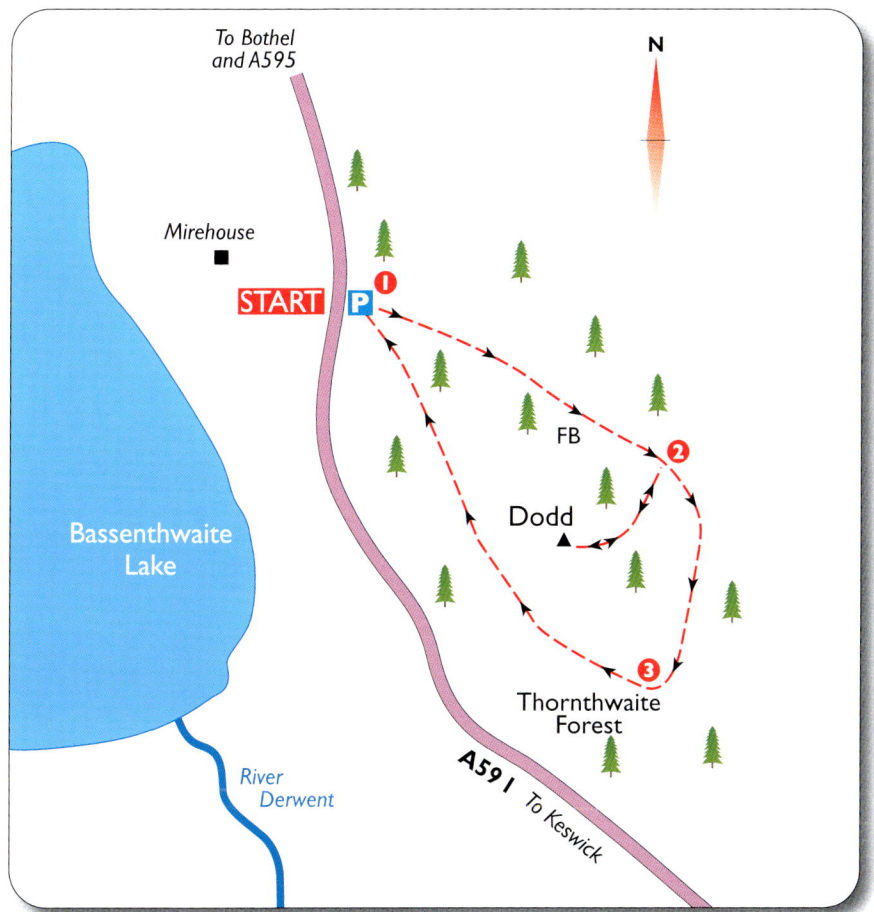

down towards a road. After dipping down, the path then starts to climb up into the woods, giving your dog off-lead time to go exploring in the trees. At this stage the route is set out by green **Forestry Commission markers** and you'll see a turning off to the right, followed by one that takes you immediately to the left. Follow this path through the woods up the hillside, with a steep drop to your left. The walk continues to follow the green markers as you climb up the steep slopes of **Dodd**. Continue straight ahead and you'll find that it levels out for a while and then starts to climb once more. Cross a footbridge and continue along the path. At this point look out for the large number of fallen trees that lie on the slope to the right. The woods really are a wonderful place to explore, with different points of interest during each

The Lake District – A Dog Walker's Guide

Wonderful views as you walk.

Dodd Fell

season, such as the varieties of fungi in late summer and autumn. When you come to a track, turn left and soon take the path off down to the right, again with green markers leading the way. This takes you over another stream on a wooden footbridge and you end up walking down the other side of the river on a level section of path, with views of **Bassenthwaite** on the right. At a T-junction of paths, turn left, following the green marker as you climb steeply and double back on your previous direction. Notice the view across the valley that opens up on the left.

2 After climbing for a while, you reach a clearing at the top. Take a well-signed path to the right towards **Dodd Summit**. As you follow the path, check out the view behind you across to **Bassenthwaite**, but then be prepared for a truly amazing vision as you climb up the path and see the scenery around **Derwent Water** unfold. Follow the forest track as it bends round to the right and winds round. You'll notice a green marker on the left identifying a brief diversion to a seat and viewpoint on the left. Continue ahead along the main path, which bends round and takes you up quite a sharp climb to the summit where there are wonderful views all around. When finished, return from the summit the way you came up. You'll see the odd pine tree up here, but it's mainly heather now, after a decision was made to clear the summit of trees. Follow the path until you reach the point where you turned off towards **Dodd Summit**. Turn right here. This forestry track bends round to the right, and you can see Keswick to the left. The track continues down, with a steep drop to the left, and slate on the right that was cut away to make the route.

3 At this point, you leave the green markers and need to keep following the track. You also leave behind the views of Derwent Water but before long you'll pick up views of Bassenthwaite Lake and the River Derwent meandering below you. Head on down by a picnic table to a signpost, where you turn right towards the **Mirehouse** and café. Pick up the green and red markers here, walking by the side of a stream. Head down steeply and you'll find yourself at the car park where you started.

2

Keswick – A Railway Walk

Boats by the side of Derwentwater.

In the northern reaches of the Lake District National Park, Keswick easily has more facilities than any other settlement, and it's also an attractive town. This walk heads out from the centre, giving maximum off-lead time for your dog and allowing you to delve into the area's industrial heritage. There are trees and undergrowth for dogs to investigate and even the odd chance to take a dip in the river.

It is now over 40 years since you could catch a train to Keswick. The days of steam engines rattling along by the foot of the fells and squeaking to a halt at the platform died when the line was included by Dr Beeching in his infamous report. Like elsewhere in the country, there are moves to get this once popular route back on track by reintroducing trains to the northern Lake District. Until that dream becomes a reality, it is possible to stretch your legs on the exact route that the trains once took. And there are several reminders

Keswick – A Railway Walk 2

of yesteryear as you head along it. You are bound to find other dog walkers on this popular route. It's a great place for dogs to exercise, and an interesting place for owners to explore. You'll follow the tracks of the once regular trains, head through tunnels, and pass, and maybe pop inside, the railway shelters that stand at the side of the track. But perhaps the greatest sight that brings home the history of this walking route are the bridges that you cross over, and there are plenty of them as the former railway ebbed and flowed over the meandering River Greta. These are known as 'bowstring' bridges, so named because of the arching iron design of the structure. But they are not all the same; keep a look out for some where the arch goes over the top of the bridge and others where it loops underneath.

Terrain
This is a level walk along an old railway line.

Where to park
There is a pay and display car park at the start of the walk in Keswick, close to the leisure centre (GR NY270238). **Map:** OS Explorer OL4 The English Lakes: North-western area.

How to get there
From Junction 40 of the M6, follow the A66 towards Keswick. Take the road towards the town and once in the central area pick up the signs for the leisure centre, which is just by the start of the walk. The pay and display car park is at the side of the hotel which now occupies the former station building.

Nearest refreshments
The walk starts and finishes close to Keswick town centre, making it easy to get to a dog-friendly pub. The popular choice is the Dog and Gun, where dogs are made very welcome. There is even a doggie menu for them to tuck into. It's at 2 Lake Road, Keswick. ☎ 01768 773463, CA12 5BT. Dogs are allowed in the whole bar area at the Pack Horse Inn, Pack Horse Court, Keswick. ☎ 01768 771148 www.packhorsekeswick.co.uk

Dog factors
Distance: 7 miles.
Road walking: None, unless you head into Threlkeld village.
Livestock: None.
Stiles: None.
Nearest vets: Millcroft Veterinary Group, Southey Hill, Keswick.

The Lake District – A Dog Walker's Guide

The Walk

1 This there-and-back walk starts from the old Keswick railway station, now a hotel. From the car park at the leisure centre you set out along the disused railway line. There are many historical elements to watch out for here and you soon find yourself on an embankment made for the line so it could be kept as level as possible. Where trains once puffed by, people and dogs can now stretch their legs and you'll soon be doing so over an old railway bridge that is the first of many over the **River Greta**. Trees on the left and right give the early stages of this walk a woodland feel and there'll be many scents for your pet to pick up. The first sign you come to informs you that you are on the old trackbed, and also that it is part of the Coast to Coast footpath. Follow signs for Threlkeld.

2 A little bit of urbanisation is encountered where the **A66** passes over the walk. Go under this huge flyover, on a purpose-built wooden passage that picks up the railway line again at the other side of the hill. Crossing a couple more bridges, you walk on wooden boarding but can see the iron structure of the original impressive engineering underneath. Cross over another bridge. The landscape changes as you move out into fields and continue through a tunnel, over another bridge. The track is very straight forward to follow. Keep on heading away from Keswick passing one of the railway workers' huts and crossing a few more bridges. The views now open up on your right, with a panorama towards St John's in the Vale beyond the A66. Follow the

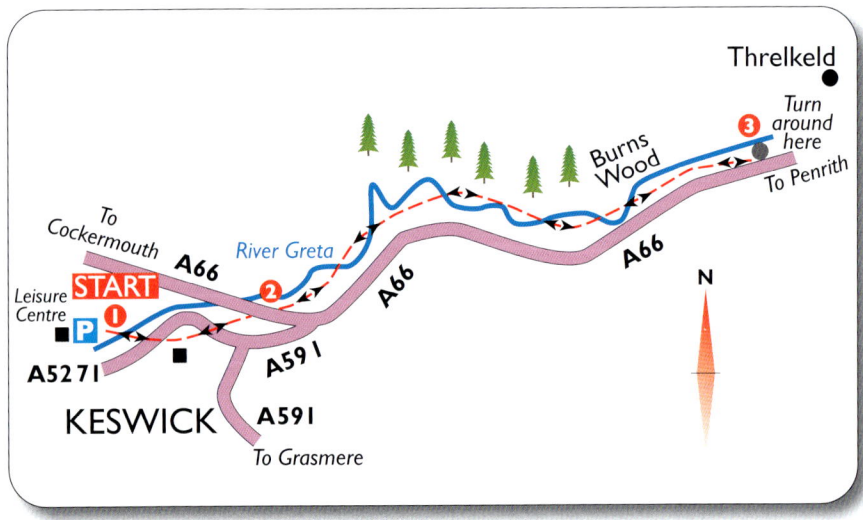

Keswick – A Railway Walk

sign to the village straight ahead, and the track will bring you out onto the A66.

3 This is as far as the disused railway track goes for walkers, so now's the time to turn around and retrace your footsteps to the starting point. Unless, that is, you fancy some light refreshments halfway through the walk. If you do, turn left onto the path by the road and then take the first left that takes you into Threlkeld village. If you keep on this main road through the village you will come to the Horse and Farrier Inn. ☎ 01768 779688 www.horseandfarrier.com CA12 4SQ

Looking along the River Greta.

Buttermere

A beautiful day at Buttermere.

Your dog will encounter water and woodland on this round walk that uses the lakeside path as well as leading through pine trees, before winding up next to a country pub.

Buttermere is nestled away in a remote valley south-west of Keswick, at the far side of the mountainous Honister Pass. Buttermere is a popular place for walkers but much quieter than the more central, easily accessible hiking bases. The name of this delightful place comes from a Norse Chieftain known as Jarl Boethar, who stamped his authority on Buttermere by naming the valley at a time when many Vikings were settling in the region. Boethar was regarded as a hero for the way he stood up for remote Cumbria against the Norman forces in the 11th century. After they invaded in 1066, the Norman army looked to spread their influence throughout England, but came up against Cumbrian resistance in the shape of natives from the north-west and Norsemen. For around half a century, they fought a guerrilla-style war against the Normans, ambushing their supplies and becoming very costly in terms of both men and money. Boethar ran such an effective campaign that local folklore told of the spilt blood of Norman soldiers giving life to the thousands of bluebells that

Buttermere (3)

grow here every spring. One section of the Norman army was based in Carlisle under the command of Ranulph les Meschines and they advanced south from Cockermouth to tackle the Cumbrian rebels. But Boethar and his men succeeded in drawing them into the side valley of Rannerdale and then routed the Normans with a surprise attack from above and behind. Today, Buttermere is a much more peaceful place, with an isolation and rugged landscape that draws people in. The lake adds to the charming and picturesque feel of this wonderful valley, a substantial stretch of water some 1½ miles long and half a mile wide. At the deepest point, Buttermere measures 90 ft – but the lake used to be much bigger. In fact, Buttermere was once connected to nearby Crummock Water and formed one long and mighty lake. But that started to silt up in the middle and over thousands of years the silt replaced the water, resulting in the two delightful lakes we see today. The history of Buttermere is explored in a few notable novels worth delving into if you want to learn more. Rosemary Sutcliffe's *The Shield Ring* from 1956 follows the life of Boethar as he makes a last stand against the Norman army, while Melvyn Bragg wrote *The Maid of Buttermere*, about the daughter of the landlord at Buttermere's Fish Inn.

Terrain
The paths are well used through the National Trust woods and by the lakeside. You may have to splash through small streams and negotiate muddy sections. There are steps and a bit of a climb.

Where to park
The pay and display car park in Buttermere village, close to the Fish Inn. (GR NY173168) **Map:** OS Explorer OL4 The English Lakes: North-western area.

How to get there
Buttermere can take a while to reach, it being further west than the more central walking areas. But, of course, that is also the appeal of the place. If heading down from Cockermouth, take the B5289 out of the town and follow

Dog factors
Distance: 2.9 miles.
Road walking: None.
Livestock: Possible on some sections. Use caution.
Stiles: None.
Nearest vets: Millcroft Veterinary Group, Wakefield Road, Cockermouth.

The Lake District – A Dog Walker's Guide

signs for Buttermere. From Keswick, take the B5289 to Seatoller and Honister, finding Buttermere after negotiating the Honister Pass.

Nearest refreshments
You can sit outside the Fish Inn, though dogs are not allowed inside. Elsewhere, try Walkers Bar at the Bridge Hotel in Buttermere, where you'll find great food and dogs are allowed. ☎ 01768 770252, www.bridge-hotel.com CA13 9UZ

The Walk
. . . .

❶ We start this lovely walk by Buttermere from the car park next to the **Fish Inn**. Beside the pub is a track that is signed down to the lake. Follow this track, bending first to the left and then to the right. Keep a look out for the waterfall

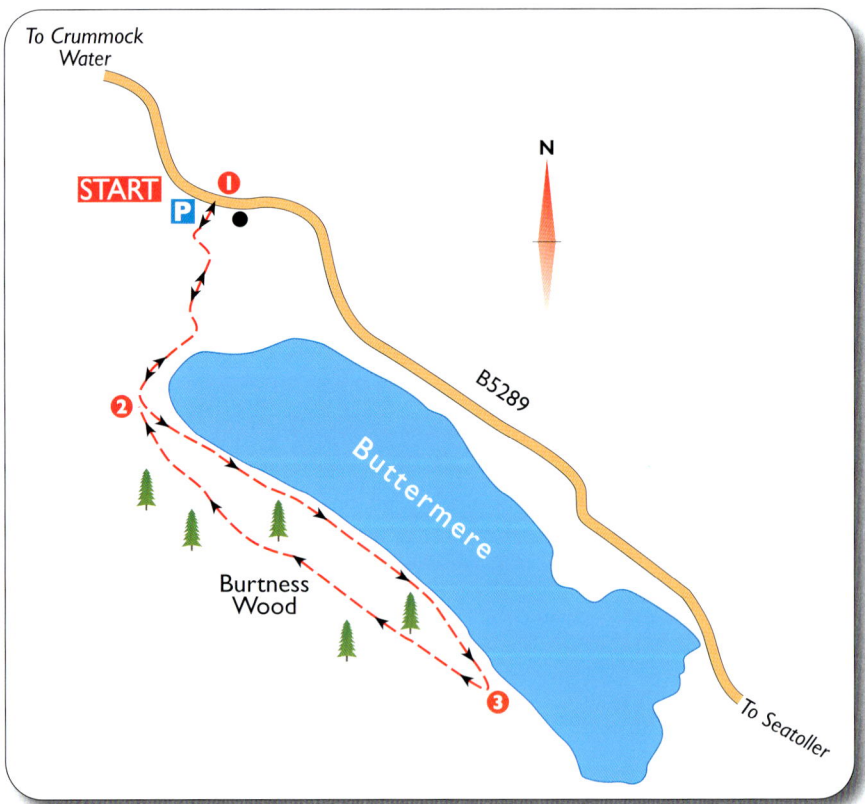

Buttermere

up to the right as **Sour Milk Gill** crashes down the hillside. Before you pass the National Trust sign for **Buttermere**, there is a bin for dog mess on the left should you need to use it. Turn right here and continue down the path, with the lake away to the left. Cross a couple of footbridges over streams flowing into the lake.

2 Make your way through a gate and turn left, to the lakeside path. This is a generally easy-access path, although sections can be a little bumpy. Your dog will love this section as it gives a chance to paddle and also roam between the pines. There are great views here over the lake towards the white house on the other side, and it's a joy to follow this section of the route as it sticks close to the water. You travel over quite a few streams feeding into Buttermere, including one that has a small wooden footbridge, and then continue straight ahead through a gate. At this point you leave the wood and enter an area of bracken with the waterfalls of **Comb Beck** up on the right.

3 Just before you get to Comb Beck and before the bridge, look out for a track on the right that doubles back on the lakeside path and heads up the hill towards the trees. Take this and begin the diagonal ascent to the wood. When you reach it, go through a gate and continue straight ahead along the track into the middle of the woods. The path forks in two; our route sticks to the left. There are several small streams to cross, one with stepping stones and others requiring you to splash through them. You can see the lake down on your right all the time as you keep pressing on along the path, which starts to climb. There's another path turning off down the hill, but whenever the lake is on your right you need to take the path on the left and stay on the hillside. You'll eventually reach a set of rocky steps down to the right. Go to the bottom of these and through a gate, then over the bridge. You now find yourself on the track you set out on. Follow this as it winds a steady way back to the pub in Buttermere.

Time to cool off on the walk.

4

Whinlatter

A sculpture of an osprey outside Whinlatter Visitor Centre.

The Forest Park at Whinlatter has a range of fantastic woodland trails and many other attractions, making it a wonderful day out for family, friends and dogs in the northern Lake District. Forests are ideal places for dogs to have safe off-lead time and there is always plenty to sniff and explore on the woodland floor.

Whinlatter Forest Park is just a short drive from Keswick. This is a fabulous Forestry Commission centre that has all the facilities you could hope for. Aside from the range of walks around the forest, some short and some stretching on for miles, there is also a café, shop, children's playground, ample parking and a toilet block, meaning that all the ingredients for some good times are here. Even if the weather's drizzly you'll find that the trees go some way to shelter you on your stroll. Whinlatter Forest Park prides itself on being the only truly

Whinlatter 4

mountain forest in England, and the views you get from the breaks in the trees are worthy of the description. The impressive outline of Skiddaw is recognisable nearby and there are also elevated views of Bassenthwaite Lake. This area is one of few in the country that are home to the native red squirrel and it's possible you may spot one high up in the trees anywhere along this walk. There are also roe deer, badgers and foxes that call this neck of the woods their home, making it a very important conservation area. If you're lucky while you're gazing up at the skies you may also catch sight of the buzzard and merlin that hunt in the forest. Even more impressive are the local osprey that head out over Whinlatter to catch fish at Bassenthwaite during their time nesting here between April and August.

Terrain
This is a relatively short walk. There are a few small but steep inclines. It is also a popular area for mountain bikes.

Where to park
There are plenty of spaces in the large pay and display car park at the Whinlatter Forest Visitor Centre (GR NY207244). **Map:** OS Explorer OL4 The English Lakes: North-western area.

How to get there
From Keswick take the A66 and head east. Take the turning on the left for Braithwaite and the follow the signs for the Whinlatter Pass. Once on the pass, climb the hill and you'll see the car park for the main visitor centre on the right.

Nearest refreshments
Refreshments are available at the Whinlatter Forest Visitor Centre, but if you fancy heading to a pub after your trek you could try the Coledale Inn at Braithwaite, originally a mill and now an excellent place to call in after local walks. ☎ 01768 778272, www.coledale-inn.co.uk CA12 5TN, or the Farmers Arms, Portinscale, near Keswick. ☎ 01768 744861, CA12 5RW, www.farmersarmspub.co.uk. Both inns welcome dogs.

Dog factors
Distance: 1.6 miles.
Road walking: None.
Livestock: None.
Stiles: None.
Nearest vets: Millcroft Veterinary Group, Southey Hill, Keswick.

The Lake District – A Dog Walker's Guide

The Walk

❶ There are several car parks around Whinlatter Forest should the recommended one be full, but this walk starts at the main pay and display parking area at the visitor centre. Walk up to the visitor centre, then pass between the buildings to the place where all the walking trails begin. We'll be following the **blue posts**, so your first move is to branch off to the left and go up into the wood. As you eventually come out of the park, the path splits in two. Follow the **blue route** off to the left further up the hill, deeper into the forest and under a canopy of pine trees. There are views over the tops of trees that open up on the right and you'll soon pass an information board about squirrels. This area is an ideal place for your dog to investigate the undergrowth and go searching through the trees. You pass a seated area that forms an outdoor classroom, further evidence of the many different ways that the forest is used by visitors, and then take the footpath off to the right, again following the **blue route**. Follow this path for a while and then take a different path off to the left, along another section that will be loved by canine companions.

❷ After a short distance the blue route goes off to the right and the red route goes straight on. Continue following the **blue path** which heads downhill and round to the right, picking up a little stream on the right that may well be dry in the summer. This section is quite steep at first but soon levels out. You cross a stream and then head over a mountain bike route before continuing along to another track. Turn left at this track and you once again head down and

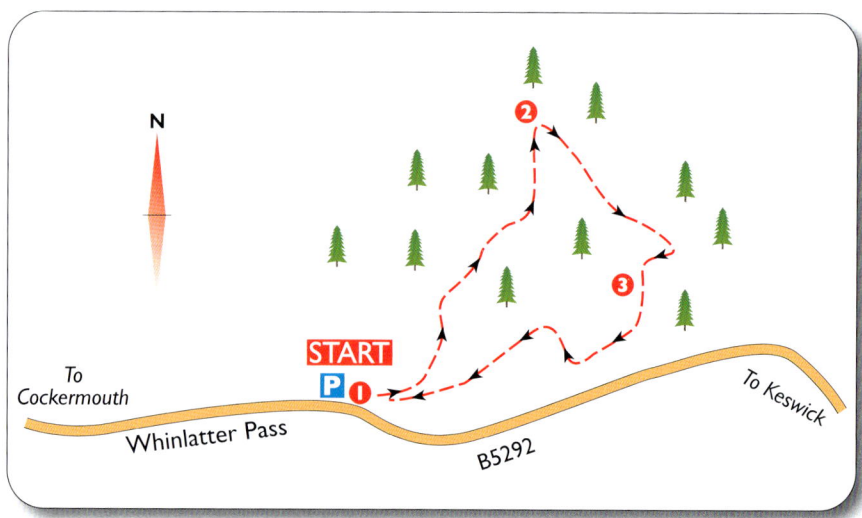

Whinlatter

follow it round to the right, soon crossing another stream where dogs will love to have a paddle. Humans, though, will love the amazing landscape of pine trees. It's quite an awesome spectacle and more like the skyline of Scotland or Canada than that which you might expect among English mountains. Head along the route, passing more little streams and eventually coming out onto another track, where you turn right and continue following the **blue markers**.

3 Then take a left and continue heading downhill, noting that the stream is getting more established. You walk by a bridge on the left, but you need to continue straight ahead, sticking to the route you're on as it bends to the right and winds upwards a little. You pass a small waterfall on your left, climb further up the track and soon pass a dam. At a track, turn right and then immediately left, almost directly opposite. This takes you uphill for a while on a fairly steep section through the woods until it brings you out of the trees and into a field. Turn left onto another track here, again following **blue markers**, and head through a gate along a track that will soon bring you back to the visitor centre.

Exploring Whinlatter Forest.

5
Ennerdale Water

Trees on the bank of Ennerdale Water.

Lakeland lovers who want a lengthy challenge for their dog cannot fail to be impressed by this gorgeous circular walk around the lake, hailed by many as the finest in the national park. As well as enjoying a longer route and some wonderful fresh air, your dog will be able to sniff around the fells and have a dip in the lake.

Ennerdale Water is one of the lesser-known gems of the Lake District, and once you've completed this circular walk you'll want to come back to it time and time again. Seasoned Lake District visitors are likely to point to Ennerdale as one of the most attractive corners of the national park. For a start, it's the

Ennerdale Water 5

only major lake without an access road alongside it. Two car parks allow you to get to the western edge of Ennerdale, but there is no access for tourist traffic at all around the shore or at the eastern edge, making this a peaceful and largely quiet escape. The remoteness of this western-most expanse of water in the Lake District contributes to the appeal of Ennerdale, and the absence of a road through the valley, combined with the fact it is not overrun by the concrete trappings of tourism, make this a wonderfully spiritual place to escape to with your dog. The position of Ennerdale Water is fabulous, surrounded by many of Cumbria's largest and finest mountains, such as Great Gable, Green Gable, High Crag, Steeple and Pillar. The lake itself is glacial in origin and measures half a mile wide by 2½ miles long. Now owned by United Utilities, it's a maximum of 45 m deep and serves 30,000 people with drinking water. To this end, the level of the lake has been artificially raised to allow it to function as a reservoir and trap more of the water that is brought in by the River Liza. There are few signs that this is drinking water, however. The serenity of the area is a match for any other Cumbrian lake and the habitat provided by the shoreline has led to Ennerdale being classified as a Site of Special Scientific Interest. It also appealed to film-maker Danny Boyle when he was location-searching for *28 Days Later*. The remote valley made a suitably spooky backdrop for this zombie movie and the closing scenes were shot around here, including a panoramic view of the lake itself. If you're feeling in a romantic mood as you trek around the lake, you're in good company. This is where former United States President Bill Clinton proposed to his girlfriend, Hillary, in 1973.

Terrain
The perimeter path that encircles Ennerdale Water is easy-going in most places, though at times it can be as tough as climbing and descending an actual fell. So care is needed, especially in the first section close to Angler's Crag.

Dog factors
Distance: 7.3 miles.
Road walking: None.
Livestock: A sensible approach is required and dogs should be kept under control as sheep may be encountered during this walk at the base of several fells.
Stiles: None.
Nearest vets: West Lakeland Veterinary Group, 55 Main Street, Egremont.

The Lake District – A Dog Walker's Guide

Where to park
The Bleach Green car park, Ennerdale (GR NY085153). **Map:** OS Explorer OL4 The English Lakes: North-western area.

How to get there
Ennerdale is in the north-west of the Lake District and so will probably take you longer to reach than the more central locations, depending on where you're travelling from obviously. If you're coming from outside the Lakes, your best bet is to leave the M6 at Junction 40 and follow the signs for Keswick, then continue to Cockermouth where you pick up the A5086 for Cleator Moor. Look out for a sign on the left to Ennerdale Bridge and from there follow signs for Ennerdale and the Bleach Green car park.

Nearest refreshments
The Fox and Hounds at Ennerdale Bridge is the nearest pub and is a lovely place to relax after a walk around this wonderful lake. The pub was bought by villagers in 2011 and the owners welcome walkers with muddy boots and dogs. ☎ 01946 861373 www.foxandhoundsinn.org CA23 3AR. Meanwhile, the Brook Inn at Cleator is a small terraced pub a little further away with a warm welcome for dog owners. ☎ 01946 811635, CA23 3DX, www.thebrookinncleator.co.uk

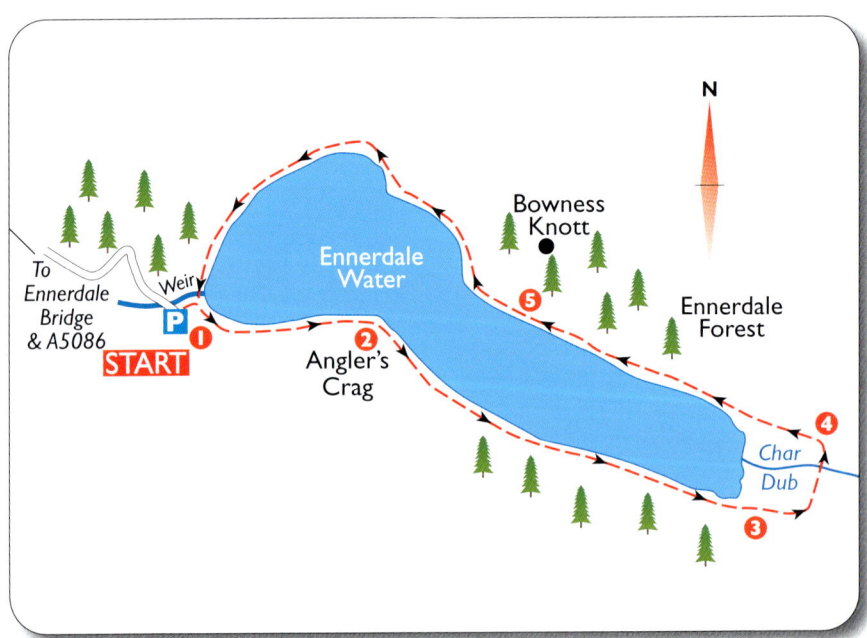

Ennerdale Water 5

The Walk

1 From the Bleach Green car park, take the path that heads for the lakeside, passing a donations box on the way down. When you get to the lake you will be presented with a choice of paths; take the one on the right and follow it as it sticks close to the water's edge. Head through a gate signalling the start of the National Trust's land at **Angler's Crag** and follow the path straight on, keeping the water just by you on the left. This first section of the walk around Angler's Crag is undoubtedly the toughest part of the walk and will involve some scrambling over rocks and walking by scree slopes. It should go without saying that great care is needed on this section, but there it is, I've said it anyway.

2 There are some tricky up and down sections, and in places I was pretty much on all fours, which will make your dog feel a bit more at home. So this section is like a proper fell climb, but as I've said it doesn't last for long, and soon you'll find yourself walking along a much more gentle section among ferns and grass. The path can still be rocky though, as you head through a gate and enjoy a section of the amble where dogs will love to take a splash and root around in the ferns. There are silver birches and a selection of other trees in the woodland as you make your way over Red Beck along rocky paths. You

Daffodils on a spring day.

The Lake District – A Dog Walker's Guide

can't help but notice the inspiring and awesome peaks and screes across the other side of the valley, these being Bowness Knott, Great Borne and Starling Dodd. The way that they encase this valley makes the scenery even more monumental. The path takes you through another gate and back down to the water. Eventually you take some stepping stones to cross a stream. Heading through a gate, you'll find yourself leaving the National Trust land known as **The Side** towards the end of Ennerdale Water, before crossing over for the return journey.

❸ Keep following the path straight on, moving away from the water. You'll soon come to a track which heads left. Follow this as it crosses **Char Dub**. Passing the eastern end of Ennerdale, you have a wonderful view off to the right as the valley rises up towards Red Pike, Pillar and Grey Crags.

❹ Our walk, however, is much more gentle, so turn left when you reach the track at the other side of the bridge. Because it's built for occasional works access, you'll notice straight away that this track is easier going. On the first section you can see that the river runs over the wall and down to the left, but then it opens up to the lake once more. There are several benches and picnic opportunities on this stretch, which passes streams heading into the lake such as Smithy Beck and Dry Beck.

❺ There is a path on the left that you need to take, but it's not well marked so make sure you notice when the track has a more substantial surface, because just before this point the new path leads down to the waterside once more. There are some rocky places on this section, and a few small climbs, but eventually you go through a gate and reach a flat path that runs at the side of the lake. This takes you on over a footbridge and along a gravel path, where your dog can have a splash in the water. It's a simple path to follow, turning left through a gate but all the while sticking to the side of the water. At this point, it's interesting to glance across to the other side and see the crags that caused an obstacle at the start of the walk. You'll be able to see the place where you're heading to before long. Keep on the lakeside path, heading through another gate and taking the left option when faced with a fork in the path. You'll pass a bench followed by a gate and then a footbridge, closely followed by a very similar bench-gate-footbridge combo. Another fork in the path appears, where you again need to take the left option, and soon you'll be crossing over the bridge to the place you set out from. Turn right at the other side of the river and head back to the car park.

6

Cleator Moor

Exploring Cleator Moor.

Around a lake and along a disused railway line, you'll find plenty of dog walkers out for a stroll in this hugely popular place for canine exercise on the western edges of the Lake District, close to Egremont. This walk was recommended by a local pet owner on Twitter and once I arrived at the starting point, I could certainly see why. The route does require you to keep your dogs on a lead for a section and there is a small amount of time spent on roads, but there is also enough scope to be off lead in woods and water to wear out even the most energetic of dogs.

The Lake District – A Dog Walker's Guide

You won't find the small Cumbrian town of Cleator Moor mentioned in many guidebooks, but if you're a dog owner there are a couple of good reasons to stop off and enjoy the nearby wooded walk around Longlands Lake. Many walkers who pass through this settlement of around 7,000 people are attempting something a lot grander than the gentle stroll described here. Cleator Moor, you see, is one of the first destinations on the Coast to Coast Walk, which starts in nearby St Bees and guides participants along the 191-mile cross-section of England to Robin Hood's Bay on the eastern shore. Devised by legendary Lake District wanderer Alfred Wainwright in the 1970s, the long-distance path takes in three national parks.

Cleator Moor developed on the back of the iron ore industry in the 19th century, which led to the building of two railway lines here. It has not been without its problems, though; subsidence has led to several buildings being destroyed, including a local school. In the 20th century the clothing company Kangol was founded in Cleator in 1938 by Jakob Spreiregen. Signs on the main road still invite you to pop into the Kangol Factory Shop, but it closed down in 2009 and the once thriving and innovative factory was abandoned. Today, most people in the area work at the nearby Sellafield energy complex, although on this walk you will enjoy an insight into the Cleator of the past by trekking down the old railway line on which local industry and workers once depended.

Terrain
These are all well-established paths with no significant climbs, making it a gentle country stroll around the western edges of Cumbria.

Where to park
There is a free car park at Longlands Lake, which is off the A5086, just south of Cleator and north of Egremont (GR NY013129). **Maps:** OS Explorer OL4 The English Lakes: North-western area, or OS Explorer 303 Whitehaven and Workington.

Dog factors
Distance: 2.3 miles.
Road walking: A short section halfway round, and a busier road to negotiate near the end of the walk to return to Longlands Lake.
Livestock: Possible in the riverside section of the walk.
Stiles: None.
Nearest vets: West Lakeland Veterinary Group, 55 Main Street, Egremont.

Cleator Moor 6

How to get there

The western edges of the Lake District can be tricky to get to and it can take longer than you think, so allow time to reach the start here. Heading from the south, take the A595 and continue north beyond Ravenglass. From the north, take the A66 from Keswick and again aim for the A595, turning south and driving beyond Whitehaven. Egremont and Cleator Moor are signed from the A595 and between the two you will see signs for Longlands Lake, off the A5086.

Nearest refreshments

The Brook Inn at Cleator is a small terraced pub with a warm welcome for dog owners. ☎ 01946 811635, CA23 3DX, www.thebrookinncleator.co.uk . The Manor House Hotel is a little further away at St Bees, but allows dogs into the lower bar and again offers meals. ☎ 01946 820587 www.manorhousestbees.co.uk CA27 0DE

The Walk

1 From the car park at Longlands Lake, head straight along the path towards the water. You'll see a bridge on the left which crosses the **River Ehen**, the river that emerges from Ennerdale Water further upstream, which is the focus of another glorious dog route (Walk 5). Cross over the bridge and follow the path straight ahead, following the sign for the lakeside walk. Here there is ample opportunity for dogs to roam around the nearby trees and take a dip in the water. There are occasional gates to pass through on this first section of the walk, but no stiles. It's almost as if it had been designed with the dog walker in mind and you'll surely see plenty of others on the way. Continue around the edge of Longlands Lake and eventually move slightly away from the water. From here you can see some industrial workings of an old mine. At this point you have a choice of how to structure the rest of the walk; you're about to enter a section of the walk which requires leads so if your dog has been enjoying the time around the water you can turn right here and go for another circuit of the lake. Or maybe a couple more!

2 Eventually, whether it's on your first or third time around the lake, when you reach the old workings you need to head straight on over the footbridge, following the path through the gate onto fields. The path sticks close to the River Ehen along this fairly straightforward section of the walk, heading through gates between the fields. As you progress through the fields you'll be able to see **Briscoe Mill Bridge** ahead of you on the left as the path brings you out onto a road.

3 Turn right and head uphill, following the road around to the left when you

The Lake District – A Dog Walker's Guide

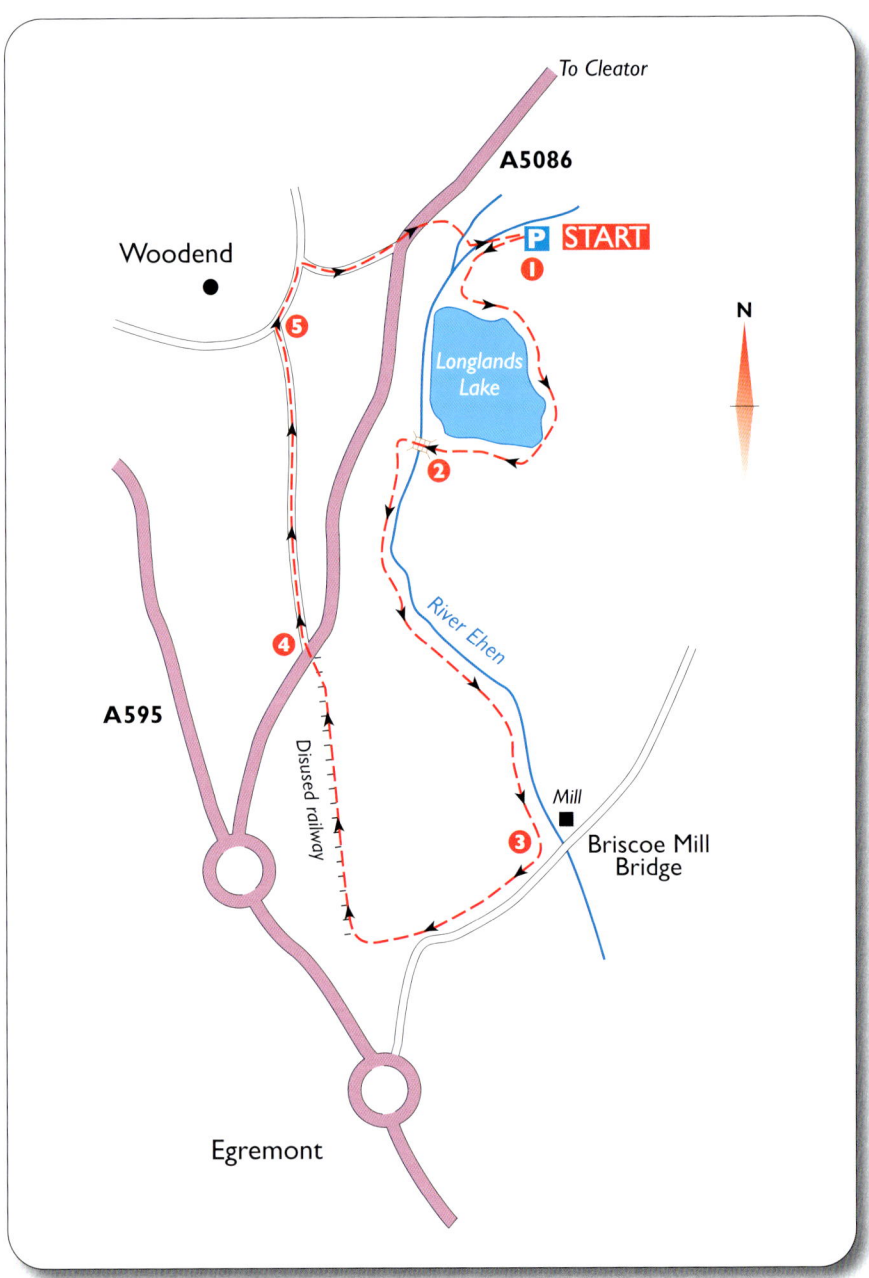

Cleator Moor

reach the top. Not long after, take a footpath on the right. This is national cycle trail 72 and it soon takes a sharp bend to the right and follows the route of a disused railway line. Once again, there's off-lead time here and a chance for your four-legged friend to explore.

4 At the end of this disused railway section you cross a bridge to reach a small country road, where you turn right. There is a dog-waste bin here. The tree-lined route is generally very quiet. After a while you'll come to some houses, from where you can see Longlands Lake down to the right. After a few twists and turns, you come to a road junction with a grassy area and a bench on the left.

5 Turn right onto **Dalzell Street** and follow this road as it bends right and brings you to another junction, where you turn left onto the **A5086**. Cross over to the other side of the road to use the pavement and follow the road for a short time until you see the sign for Longlands Lake on the right. Take this road past a couple of industrial units to arrive back at the car park where you started.

Nose to the ground!

The Bowder Stone

There is a great view from the top of Bowder Stone.

A short stroll along an easy access path with a place to let your dog play by the river. This is an excellent excursion if you don't want to make a full afternoon of it, possibly giving yourself an extra place to stop off after finishing the walks at Dodd Fell (Walk 1) or Buttermere (Walk 3).

If it wasn't for the signs pointing it out and the ladder fixed in position to take walkers to the top, you could quite easily wander by the Bowder Stone without picking up on its significance. You'd perhaps stop and stare at it and remark on how large it was, but you'd probably conclude that this was just another boulder that had tumbled down the hillside from the surrounding fells. But you may be wrong; many believe that the Bowder Stone is made of a rock type that is not typical of this part of the Lake District. The theory goes that this is a glacial erratic; a rock that is not native to the

The Bowder Stone

surroundings and has been transported from its original place by an ice sheet during the last Ice Age. It is widely believed that the 2,000 ton Bowder Stone was actually transported over many miles from Scotland and deposited in the current Borrowdale setting. When you stare at it, contemplating this monstrously impressive natural removal, the Bowder Stone stops being 'just a boulder' and becomes more a work of art, a reflection of an awesome process of nature. The theory of the Bowder Stone's history, however, is contested. An alternative idea suggests this 30 ft giant, thought to be 4 million years old, is made up of volcanic rock possibly found elsewhere in the valley and so could have had origins a lot closer to Borrowdale than Scotland. The area, like many parts of the Lake District, is owned and maintained by the National Trust, though at one time it was the property of local gent John Pocklington, who purchased it in 1798. It was he who first put a ladder on the Bowder Stone so visitors could climb to the top, although back then there were plenty of travellers who avoided Borrowdale entirely because of the large boulders that were strewn over the valley and gave it a wild appearance. The fear of the valley did not last too long, though, and before long the Bowder Stone was becoming a hot destination for artists who wanted to capture the unique beauty of its place in the surrounding valley. Perhaps the most famous interpretation came from Victorian painter John Atkinson Grimshaw, who depicted it in a romantic style, now held as part of the Tate Collection. Others who regularly come to the Bowder Stone are climbers, many of whom attempt to scale parts of it using chalk on their hands to enhance their grip. Part of the ground around the stone has been dug away to make this more of a challenge.

Terrain
Some steps to negotiate and a road to cross, but the path is generally level and accessible.

Where to park
The National Trust's Bowder Stone car park on the B5289 (GR NY253168).
Map: OS Explorer OL4 The English Lakes: North-western area.

Dog factors
Distance: 1.1 miles.
Road walking: One road to cross.
Livestock: None.
Stiles: None.
Nearest vets: Millcroft Veterinary Group, Southey Hill, Keswick.

The Lake District – A Dog Walker's Guide

Space to splash and play.

The Bowder Stone 7

How to get there

Leave the M6 at Junction 40 and head for Keswick. When you reach the town, follow the B5289 south towards Rosthwaite, Seatoller and Honister.

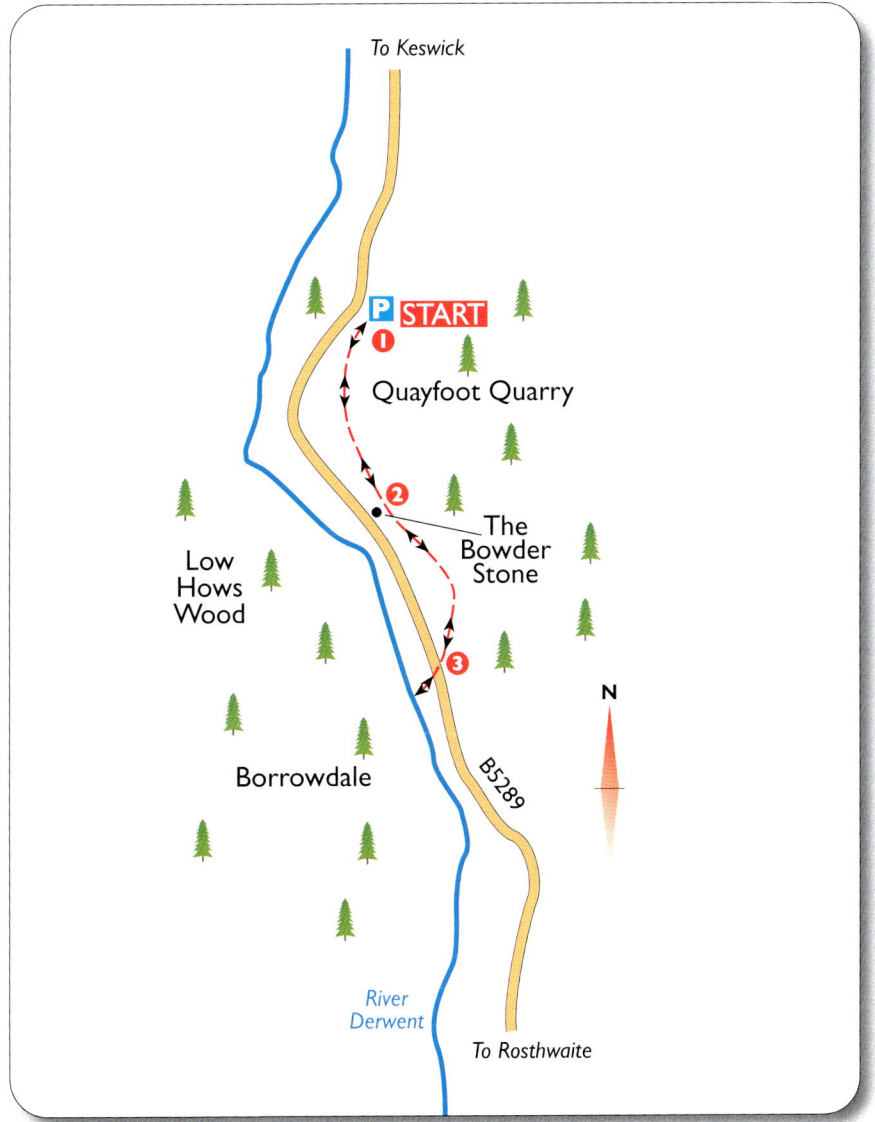

The Lake District – A Dog Walker's Guide

Nearest refreshments

Dogs are allowed in the bar at Mary Mount Hotel, in Borrowdale. ☎ 01768 777223, CA12 5UU, www.marymounthotel.co.uk. The Swinside Inn in the Newlands Valley is also a welcoming venue. ☎ 01768 778253, CA12 5UE, www.swinsideinn.com

The Walk

❶ From the car park head towards the pay and display machine and you'll see a sign pointing you in the direction of the **Bowder Stone**. Head down the steps that take you towards the road. Before reaching the road, however, you will see the NT Bowder Stone sign off to the left and you need to follow this. From the outset, the views are amazing and you will enjoy the sight of crags across the other side of Borrowdale, including Low Scawdel, Eel Crags and Nitting Haws. You'll soon pass the site of the disused **Quayfoot Quarry** on the left, now sealed off due to its dangers but you may see organised groups taking part in abseiling lessons. Head through a wooden gate after you've gone beyond the quarry and you now enter a small wood, with the path continuing on ahead. There are rocks now sloping up to the left, and again you may see groups climbing up these.

❷ But the real rocky attraction here is the Bowder Stone and it comes into view ahead of you, a huge boulder that has steps attached to it so you can get up to the top. Be sure to do this, just to get a feel for the size of it, but do take care as the steps are steep. You're likely to see people making an altogether more difficult ascent of the Bowder Stone as it's a popular challenge for climbers. Head beyond the stone and continue on the track, through the woods, until it brings you out at the road.

❸ Put your dog on a lead, cross over here and head through the gap in the wall to access a great place for your dog to play in the **River Derwent**. When you have finished, put your dog back on a lead before heading back to the road and take the same easy-going path back to the car park.

8

Patterdale

An Ullswater steamer at Glenridding.

Taking you to the southern shores of Ullswater, this great Lake District dog walk offers fantastic views from Silver Point. There is also water for your dog to play in and woods filled with interesting scents.

Ullswater is typical of many long, narrow stretches of water in Cumbria. It is a ribbon lake created during the ice age when the glacier gradually scooped out the bottom of the valley and filled the area with meltwater. And yet the shape of Ullswater singles it out from others in the area and also offers more clues as to how it formed. If you look at Ullswater on a map it has been created in a Z formation – three distinct sections that allow it to bend around the mountains. This is because it was formed by three glaciers, all working on different sections and eventually coming together to make the Ullswater we know today. It measures around 9 miles long and ¾ of a mile wide, while the deepest spot in the lake reaches down 63 metres. What we're a little more unsure about is how the lake came to get the name Ullswater. Popular theories are that there was a Viking chief named Ulf who gave the lake its name, and also that it came from the Viking word for wolf (ulfr) due to the wolves living in this neck of the woods during days gone by. Today the lake is a very popular

The Lake District – A Dog Walker's Guide

destination for tourists and many believe Ullswater to be the most beautiful of all the lakes. Certainly, if you take a trip on one of the famous Ullswater Steamers, it can be difficult to disagree with this assertion.

Terrain
Rocky paths but easy to follow.

Where to park
There is limited off-road parking in Patterdale, or use the pay and display car park by the White Lion pub (GR NY396158). **Map:** OS Explorer OL5 The English Lakes: North-eastern area.

How to get there
From Junction 40 of the M6, head towards Keswick on the A66. At the first roundabout, take the exit left on the A592. Patterdale is at the far, southern end of Ullswater.

Nearest refreshments
Dogs are welcome at the Travellers Rest, at nearby Glenridding. ☎ 01768 482298, CA11 0QQ. In the other direction at Brotherswater, dogs are welcome at the Brotherswater Inn if kept on a lead. ☎ 01768 482239, CA11 0NZ, www.sykeside.co.uk/inn

Dog factors
Distance: 7 miles.
Road walking: Part of the route is on a track gaining access to a campsite.
Livestock: Some of the route is fenced off, but there is always the chance of encountering sheep, so use caution.
Stiles: None.
Nearest vets: Frame, Swift and Partners, Carleton, Penrith.

The Walk

1 Leave the village passing the **White Lion** pub on your left and take the road that turns off to the left. Cross the bridge then immediately take the path that heads off to the left at the side of the beck.

2 Head through a kissing gate and keep the beck on the left, with a fence on the right. Through another gate, you head into some woods and when you pass

Patterdale 8

through another gate turn right on the track towards the farm. Go past the cattle grid using the gate on the right.

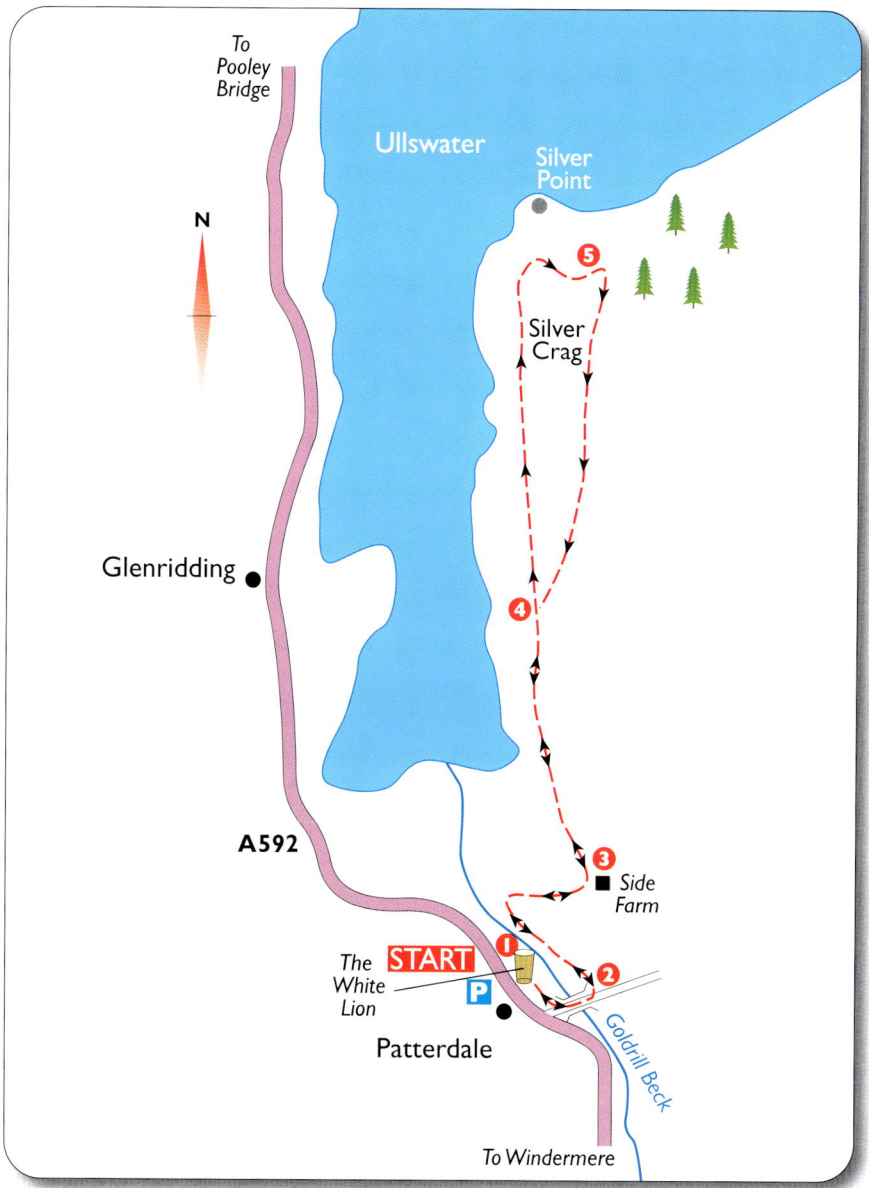

The Lake District – A Dog Walker's Guide

③ You'll soon find yourself at **Side Farm**, which is a popular place in summer with a tea shop and nearby campsite. Go through the courtyard and turn left onto the track, heading through a gate. At this point you may encounter some sheep so keep an eye out and use a lead if necessary. This is a steady, simple track to follow and soon you'll start to see great views of Ullswater down to your left, with fells rising up at the other side of the valley.

④ At a fork in the path bear left and so continue on the track overlooking the lake. Keep along this and soon you will find yourself with a fine view over Silver Point. It's a great spot to rest and have a picnic - in good weather, at any rate.

⑤ Continue on the path as it bends around to the right. Before you reach the woods turn right (GR 397182) and follow this path as it rises over the hill and dips down the other side. After around half a mile you will spot a path heading downhill to the right. Take this and join the original path at the bottom, turning left onto it and completing the loop around Silver Crag. From here it's a case of retracing your footsteps, so proceed along the track until you come to Side Farm, turn right here and walk through the farm. Continue ahead along the track and just before you reach the beck, turn left onto the path that goes by the waterside. Through the wood and out of the gate at the far end, cross the bridge on the right and head back to the main road. Turn right, back to the car park.

Stopping to admire the view.

Thirlmere

A peaceful day at Thirlmere.

The fells around Thirlmere are wonderful places to explore, offering splendid scenery and a sense of calm that is missing from those lakes more popular with tourists. Walkers start their ascent of Helvellyn from here, but you may be pleased to learn that this is a far gentler stroll! The area is an ideal spot for dogs, with trees, bushes and mosses to explore – and a river by the path at the start.

What is the history of Thirlmere? Before 1890 there were two lakes occupying this central stretch of the Lake District. They were Leathes Water and Wythburn Water, but the decision was made to build a dam to create a much larger reservoir in order to quench the thirst of the population in Manchester. The official opening ceremony took place in 1894 after four years of construction. The idea dated back to the 1870s, when it became clear that there was soon going to be a supply issue for the growing Manchester population, who were at that time relying on the Longdendale Reservoirs – a walk around this is featured in my *Peak District Dog Walker's Guide*. The preferred source of water was initially Ullswater, but it was later decided to build a dam and create Thirlmere, even though there was quite a lot of local opposition to the scheme to raise the water level in the valley.

The reservoir, which pretty much runs north to south in the valley, was an

The Lake District – A Dog Walker's Guide

amazing feat of Victorian engineering. The plan was to transport millions of gallons of water from the north-western hills to the city every day. To allow this to happen, a remarkably ambitious 96-mile aqueduct was built, which remains the longest in the country. Water from Thirlmere arrives in Manchester after about a day, with no need for pumps along the way as the whole process relies on gravity. The carefully measured aqueduct drops down by about 20 inches every mile, allowing the water to flow down at speeds in the region of 4 miles an hour. Our walk goes close to Dunmail Raise, a challenging section of the aqueduct that required a lengthy tunnel to be dug. Two 19th-century mining teams tackled the tunnel, approaching it from different ends and – amazingly – they were only 8 inches out when they met.

Terrain
The paths are easy to follow but note that there are a few steep climbs on this one.

Where to park
The Wythburn pay and display car park near Wythburn chapel on the A591 between Grasmere and Keswick, (GR NY324136). **Map:** OS Explorer OL5 The English Lakes: North-eastern area.

How to get there
From Keswick join the main A591 running north to south through the Lake District. Follow the signs to Windermere and the car park will be on the left at the southern end of Thirlmere. If you're coming from the south, head to Keswick from Grasmere and look for the parking area on the right.

Nearest refreshments
For a dog-friendly pub, try the King's Head Inn, Thirlmere, where dogs are welcome in the bar. ☎ 01768 772393, CA12 4TN. In nearby Borrowdale you will find Mary Mount Hotel ☎ 01768 777223, www.marymounthotel.co.uk CA12 5UU.

Dog factors
Distance: 1.8 miles.
Road walking: A short distance on a track to the car park.
Livestock: None.
Stiles: None.
Nearest vets: Millcroft Veterinary Group, Southey Hill, Keswick.

Thirlmere 9

The Walk

1 With your back to the road, head over to the left-hand side of the car park and go through a gate. Turn right and begin a short, sharp climb up the hill. With

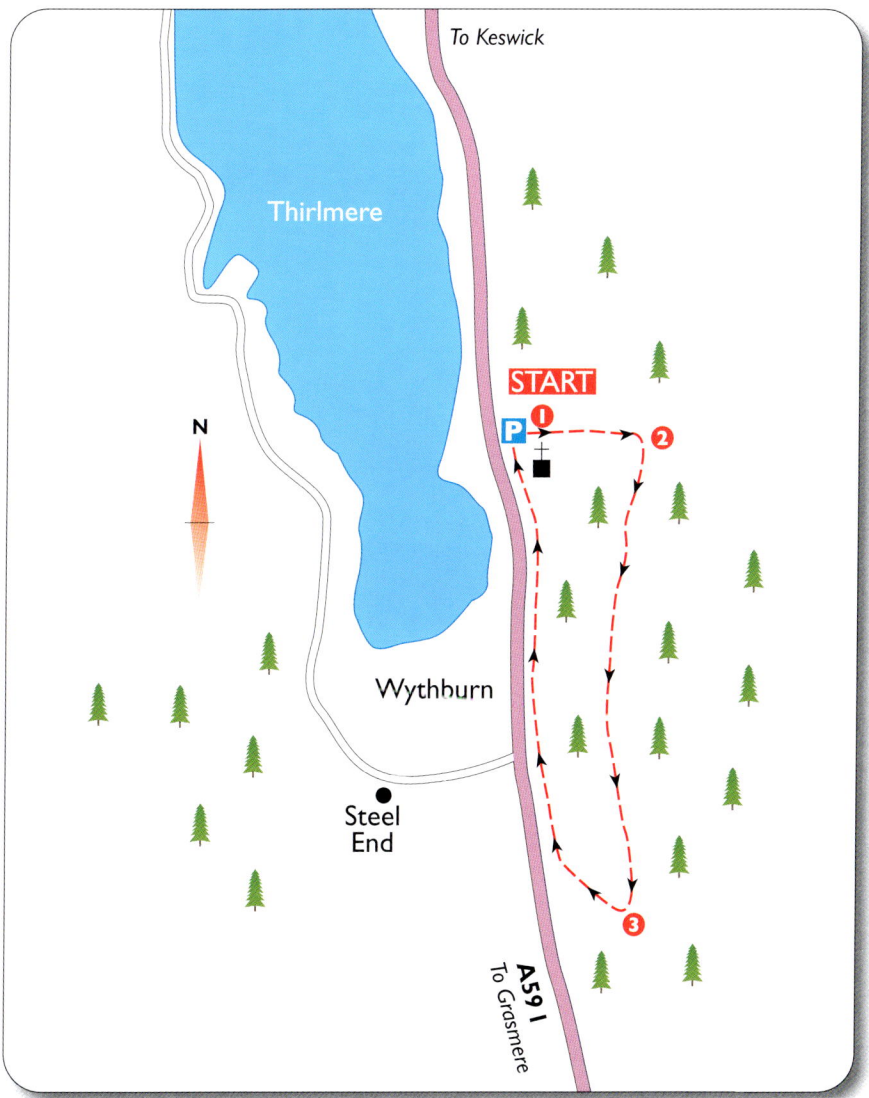

The Lake District – A Dog Walker's Guide

a river running on the left, this is a steep path and a strenuous start to the walk, entering woods and filling your lungs with the wonderful smell of pine trees. Soon you will start to climb on a stone-cobbled path.

2 When you reach a track, turn right and follow the signs for **Dunmail Raise**. Straight away the route levels out for a much more leisurely stroll. Down through the pine trees to the right you can see **Thirlmere**. As Thirlmere is a reservoir, this land is owned by United Utilities and the routes through it are permissive footpaths. The route continues along this path as the trees on the right start to thin out, allowing more of a view on the right that takes in the fells across the valley and the farm down at Steel End. Continue ahead, over a stream and beyond a gate.

3 Eventually you come out of the trees and the path dips down and to the right. Stick to this main track and at the bottom go through a gate. Continue straight ahead on the track as it begins to slowly dip down towards the main road. Instead of going onto the road, take the path off to the right following the sign for the **Thirlmere Loop**. This takes you into the woods once more, through a kissing gate and then over a number of small streams via footbridges, with the water flowing beneath you into Thirlmere. Be aware that the road is close by on the left and in places here the path becomes narrow. After a while this path brings you out onto a gravel track, where you turn left and continue over a couple of footbridges. The route enters thick and dark woodland. Continue ahead to reach another track where you turn right, back to the car park.

Setting off on a woodland adventure.

Kentmere

A beautiful day at Kentmere.

A walk up and down a remote valley along both sides of the River Kent. There are some impressive fells and crags to view, and time for your dog to enjoy a splash in the river. This walk is a favourite with local dog owners and so it's a good opportunity for your dog to socialize. You'll find plenty for you both to investigate.

Terrain
Some fairly steep climbs, but nothing too strenuous.

Where to park
Parking is limited at Kentmere, so I would advise getting there early. There is some parking by the church (GR NY456041), but on some occasions a local farmer also opens up a field and allows cars to be left if you contribute £3 to an honesty box. **Map:** OS Explorer OL7 The English Lakes: South-eastern area.

The Lake District – A Dog Walker's Guide

How to get there
Kentmere is one of the nearest Lakeland valleys to Kendal and so is very accessible. Leave the M6 at Junction 36 and follow the signs to Kendal, later picking up the A591 to Windermere. Keep an eye out for a turning on the right towards Staveley and Kentmere. Drive through Staveley and follow the signs for Kentmere, heading up the long valley road to the parking spaces near the church.

Nearest refreshments
At Staveley, try the Gateway Inn, on Crook Road, which is dog-friendly and has a large outdoor area. ☎ 01539 724187, www.gatewayinn-cumbria.co.uk LA8 8LX. Or you could follow the signs for Hawkshead Brewery to find a bar serving meals and places to sit outside. ☎ 01539 825260, www.hawksheadbrewery.co.uk LA8 9LR

Dog factors
Distance: 6 miles.
Road walking: Some, mainly on farming roads. At the start and end there are small country lanes to walk on.
Livestock: Likely to meet some en route. Common sense approach needed.
Stiles: 2 ladder stiles.
Nearest vets: Westmorland Veterinary Group, Riverside Business Park, Kendal.

The Walk

❶ Take the path to the right of the church, as you look at it from the road, signed towards Upper Kentmere. When this path forks, you should opt for the track on the right. You will have noticed as you made your way up to the start of this walk that the valley is a spectacular setting; there are dramatic crags and fells on either side, giving the valley a mystical charm. Continue on the path, passing **Rawe Cottage** on the right and heading through a farm and a gate on the other side. The track continues round to the left with the wonderful drystone walls on either side. Indeed, if you gaze up to your right you can see similar walls criss-crossing the hillside and you can only imagine the dedication of the farmer to build them on such difficult terrain. It will have been safe to have your dog off-lead so far, but you stand high chances of encountering livestock on this route so use common sense and be ready to put your pet on

Kentmere 10

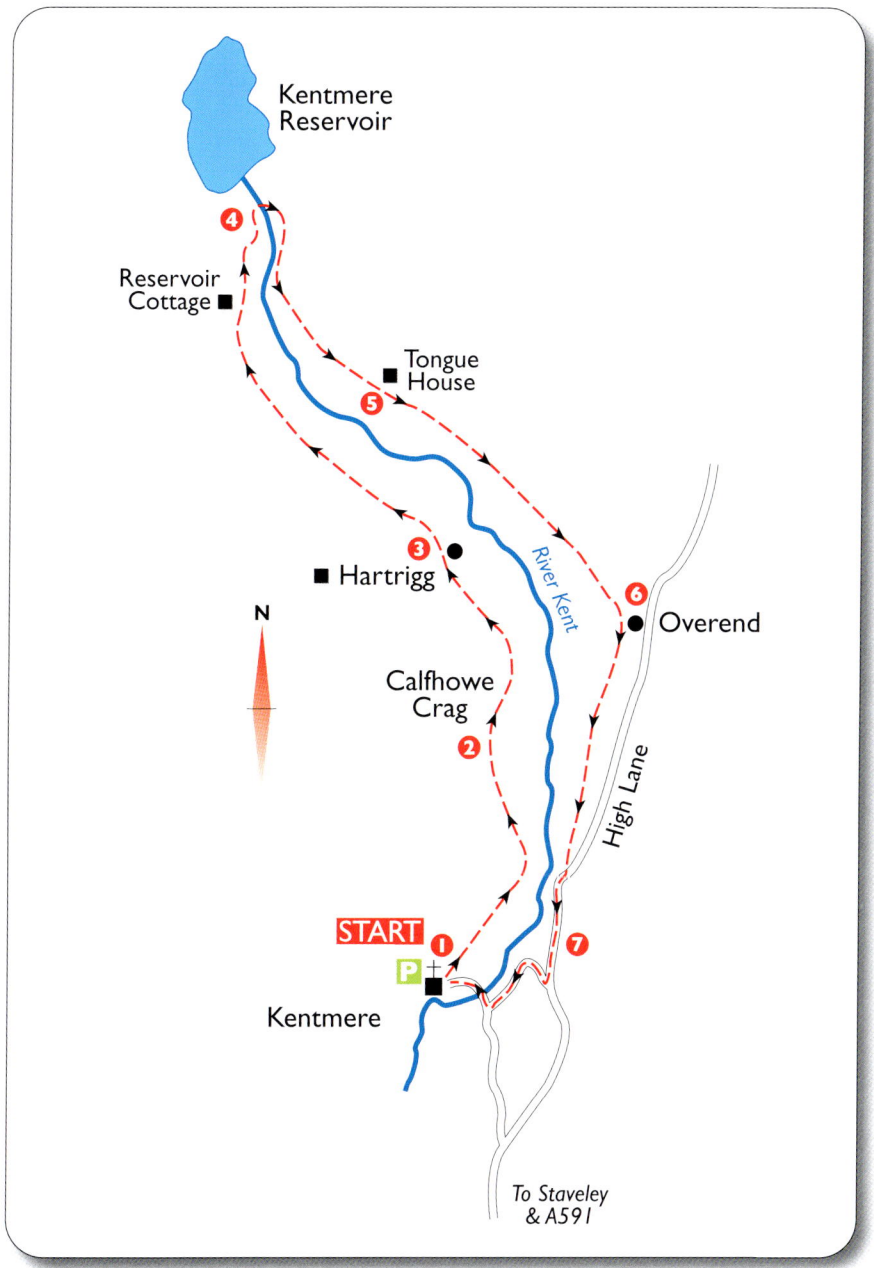

The Lake District – A Dog Walker's Guide

a lead. Continue along the track as it eventually leads into a series of fields. Go through the fields sticking to the obvious path. You will soon go through a gate and see another gate on the left side of the field, beyond which there is a road.

❷ Go through this gate and turn right onto the road. Although this is a properly surfaced road, in reality it is only for vehicles going to the farm ahead so your chances of meeting rush-hour traffic are slim. Up on the left at this point is the impressive **Calfhowe Crag**. Continue on the track beyond it, going by a farm building on your left.

❸ After about half a mile you come to the farm buildings at **Hartrigg** and the path here branches off to the left. Head through a gate and you'll see a wood on your right, with the path starting to climb a little at this point. The fells up on the left are an impressive bunch, ranging from Ill Bell to Froswick. Cross over a stream and continue ahead up the track and through a kissing gate. Soon after, go through another gate and over another stream. All the time you are working your way up to **Reservoir Cottage**. It's clear once you get here that this was once a quarrying area, with heaps of slate to be seen everywhere. Go through a kissing gate past the cottage and then continue ahead on the track, passing the piles of slate, and then just before you reach **Kentmere Reservoir** take the path off to the right.

❹ Having crossed over the river coming out of the reservoir, turn immediately right and follow the river down the upper parts of the valley, where once again there are remains of quarries. At this point you come to a tall ladder stile. Large dogs may need help to negotiate this. Continue on the easy-to-follow path as it heads down the valley.

❺ At an old farm building, **Tongue House**, go the through gates as the route bends to the left and then to the right beyond the courtyard. The path follows a drystone wall on the right before you come to the second ladder stile. Small dogs will be able to squeeze under the gate next to it. You'll soon end up walking by the river, providing a good chance for a doggy paddle. Head through another couple of gates and pass a farm building before eventually coming out at a settlement called **Overend**.

❻ The path splits in two here. Take the one on the right, known as Low Lane, with High Lane being the road up on the left. Head through a gate and when you reach a track turn right. Continue along a grassy path, crossing a stone footbridge. Cross over a stream and when you reach a signpost follow the bridleway to the right heading to Kentmere. You'll find yourself on a narrow track with woods on the left and a wall on either side. Go through

Kentmere 10

another gate, and then continue ahead to reach the road, where you turn right.

7 From here you can see the church where you started on the other side of the valley. Take the first road on the right and head downhill. This road brings you out directly opposite the farmer's field sometimes used as a car park. If you parked at the church, turn right and follow the road back.

Time for a rest at the end of the walk.

11

South Grizedale

The white waters of Force Beck.

There are plenty of walks to try out in Grizedale Forest, and not all of them set out from the visitor centre. Take this little circular stroll for example, nestling at the southern end of this fantastic forest. This area is a paradise for dogs who will love splashing in rivers, rummaging around in thick ferns and sniffing out the scents of the forest. It also offers plenty of off-lead time as you are safely away from sheep!

On your journeys around Grizedale Forest (*see also* Walk 12) you'll encounter some of the Forest Art for which it has become famous. There are dozens of sculptures for you to discover on what can be intriguing and thought-provoking walks. However, when it comes to art the Lake District is not just about sculpture. It is one of the most famed regions of the country for inspiring writers to create classic pieces of work. Among the most recognised around the world are the Lake Poets of the 19th century, and the biggest name among these is William Wordsworth. He spent most of his 80 years living among the mountains of the Lake District. On one visit to Ullswater,

South Grizedale

Wordsworth was charmed by spring daffodils and the resulting *I Wandered Lonely As A Cloud* is, to this day, one of the most well-known and loved of all the classic English poems. When it comes to famous Lake District writers, though, the biggest global phenomenon has been created by Beatrix Potter. Although not a native of the Lake District, Beatrix was born into a wealthy family and spent holidays on the shores of Windermere at Wray Castle, falling in love with the natural setting from an early age. Her repeated trips to the Lakes influenced many of her Peter Rabbit books. With the profits from her early publications, she moved to Hill Top, not far from Grizedale Forest. Hill Top is now owned by the National Trust.

Terrain
Straight forward route to follow, some parts are steep and some of the ground is rocky.

Where to park
The Forestry Commission Blind Lane car park (GR SD344912). **Map:** OS Explorer OL7 The English Lakes: South-eastern area.

How to get there
Head for Newby Bridge at the southern reaches of Windermere and then go towards Satterthwaite. When you reach Force Mills, take the road on the right and you'll see the car park on the left.

Nearest refreshments
For a good dog-friendly pub and some great Lake District walks, head to Near Sawrey, between Windermere and Esthwaite Water, where you'll find the Tower Bank Arms, made famous in the Beatrix Potter book *Jemima Puddleduck*. ☎ 015394 36334, www.towerbankarms.co.uk LA22 0LF. At close by Far Sawrey you'll find the Cuckoo Brow Inn, where dogs and muddy boots are welcome. ☎ 015394 43425, www.cuckoobrow.co.uk LA22 0LQ.

Dog factors
Distance: 2.5 miles.
Road walking: 2 roads to cross.
Livestock: None.
Stiles: None.
Nearest vets: South Lakes Veterinary Centre, Victoria Road, Ulverston.

The Lake District – A Dog Walker's Guide

The Walk

1 From the car park, look for a wooden post marking the start of the **High Bowkerstead Trail**. Straight away the path takes you steeply up into the woods, going deeper into the trees and ferns. Along this trail you are following the white marker posts. Follow them all the way to the top and then continue to follow them as the path bends round to the left. Now the path starts to drop down a little and you'll soon come to a path where you turn left and head downhill and towards the road so put your dog on a lead.

2 When you reach the road, cross straight over. Pick up the path at the other side

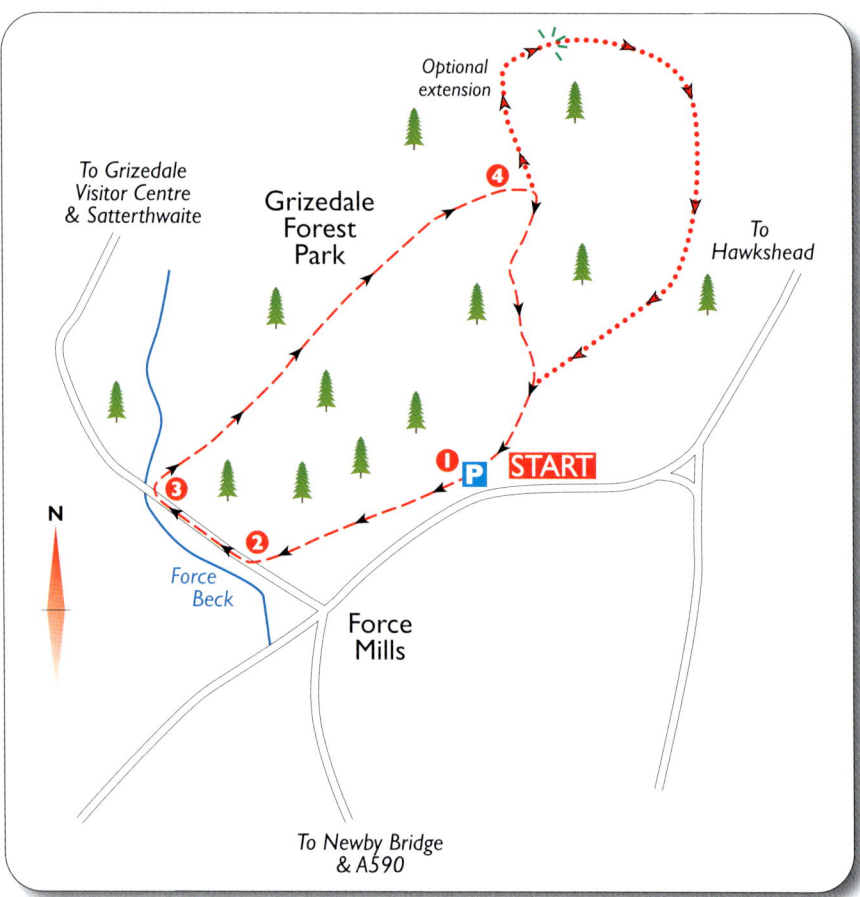

South Grizedale

by turning right and following the white markers again. You will now have **Force Beck** running by on your left. Follow the route of the river past a few small waterfalls and you'll see another white post to head for involving a bit of a scramble up and over a rock.

3 Once up there, continue ahead but keep your dog close as the path brings you out at a road once more, and again you cross straight over and pick up the route at the other side. You now continue ahead on this track, following it as it bends round to the left. Soon you'll come to a path off to the right. Turn up here, following signs for the **Bowkerstead Trail**. After a while, at a fork, take the left path. This goes uphill, bending round to the right and continuing the climb, passing a little wooden bat sculpture on the right. This section of the walk is steep and strenuous and when you do reach the top you come to a shelter that was obviously built some time ago because the views – which once would have been outstanding – are now blocked by the trees that have since grown. Follow the path to the right and you come to a small clearing where the path levels out and heads to the left. Ignore the paths going off to the left and right at this point, continue going ahead following the white markers. You will soon come out to a track, where you need to turn right and go downhill.

4 At this point, there is the option to turn left and continue on the longer **Bowkerstead Trail Route**. If you choose to do this, head left and carry on following the white posts – it adds an extra 1½ miles to the route taking you to a viewpoint after a steep climb. The shorter route heads down to the right. A good view over the rolling hills opens up on the left, I saw a deer at the edge of the woods here so keep a look out, especially at dusk. As the track bends round to the left, there is a post indicating that the route we are following cuts off to the right. Continue down on the path, through the wood and back to the car park.

Enjoying off-lead time in the forest.

Grizedale Tarn

Admiring the view across Grizedale Tarn.

Sandwiched between Coniston Water and Windermere is the vast area of Grizedale Forest, home to a wide range of wildlife as well as some unusual sculptures. There are a variety of different walks here, both long and short, and all suitable for dogs. This is a route well kitted out for dogs, with water bowls at the start and a plethora of natural features to keep them in their element on the walk. You can also relax knowing there won't be any sheep in the forest, although be aware that some of the paths are popular with mountain bikers. It is quite possible for you and your dog to spend an entire holiday exploring Grizedale's twisting woodland routes.

You could see a range of birds when you're walking on the forest trails. If you're very lucky, you might spot a buzzard, or even a red kite following a recent programme to reintroduce them. At dawn or dusk you should also be looking out for red deer, especially on the edge of the forest's clearings, as this

dale Tarn (12)

area is home to the country's only indigenous herd. But the forest routes, be they lengthy or short, will also open your eyes to a changing programme of art that helps to bring these tree-filled areas to life. Grizedale Forest was the first in the UK to welcome art and, since 1977, international artists have created pieces to complement the environment in this inspirational part of the Lake District. Linked by the cycle and walking paths that wind through so much of this forest, there are now somewhere in the region of 40 pieces of art placed in the forest and the Forestry Commission is constantly working with artists to introduce more. The ones you may encounter on this walk include the giant stile called *Concrete Country* by Lucy Tomlins, *Some Fern* by Kerry Morrison, and dating back to 1977, *The Clockwork Forest*, which wound up here in 2011. The woodland covers over 24 square km and attracts 200,000 visitors every year. The majority of these head out on foot, but around a quarter bring their bikes.

Terrain
The paths are easy to follow, some with steeper, rocky ground.

Where to park
There is a Forestry Commission pay and display car park across the road from the visitor centre (GR SD336942). **Map:** OS Explorer OL7 The English Lakes: South-eastern area. The Grizedale Visitor Centre is a good place to base yourself, there are plenty of facilities such as toilets, a café, and a shop. There is also a playground for children and a sheltered picnic area in case the weather takes a turn for the worse.

How to get there
To get to the visitor centre from the north, head for Hawkshead on the B5286 and look out for the brown signs to Grizedale when you reach the village. From the south, aim for Newby Bridge and turn off the A590 here. Cross over the railway bridge and turn left, following the road round before taking the next left and then a right turn. Head towards Rusland and then towards Hawkshead, picking up the signs for Grizedale on the way.

Dog factors
Distance: 3.5 miles.
Road walking: One road to cross.
Livestock: None.
Stiles: None.
Nearest vets: Oak Hill Vet Group, 1 Church Street, Ambleside.

The Lake District – A Dog Walker's Guide

Nearest refreshments

The nearest settlement of any size to Grizedale Forest is Hawkshead, where there are a few pubs that welcome dogs. Try the Kings Arms Hotel in The Square. ☎ 01539 436372 www.kingsarmshawkshead.co.uk LA22 0NZ and the Queen's Head on Main Street. ☎ 01539 436271 www.queensheadhawkshead.co.uk LA22 0NS. To take a taste of the area home, you could visit Hawkshead Relish in The Square, where they sell a range of fantastic pickles and preserves. www.hawksheadrelish.com

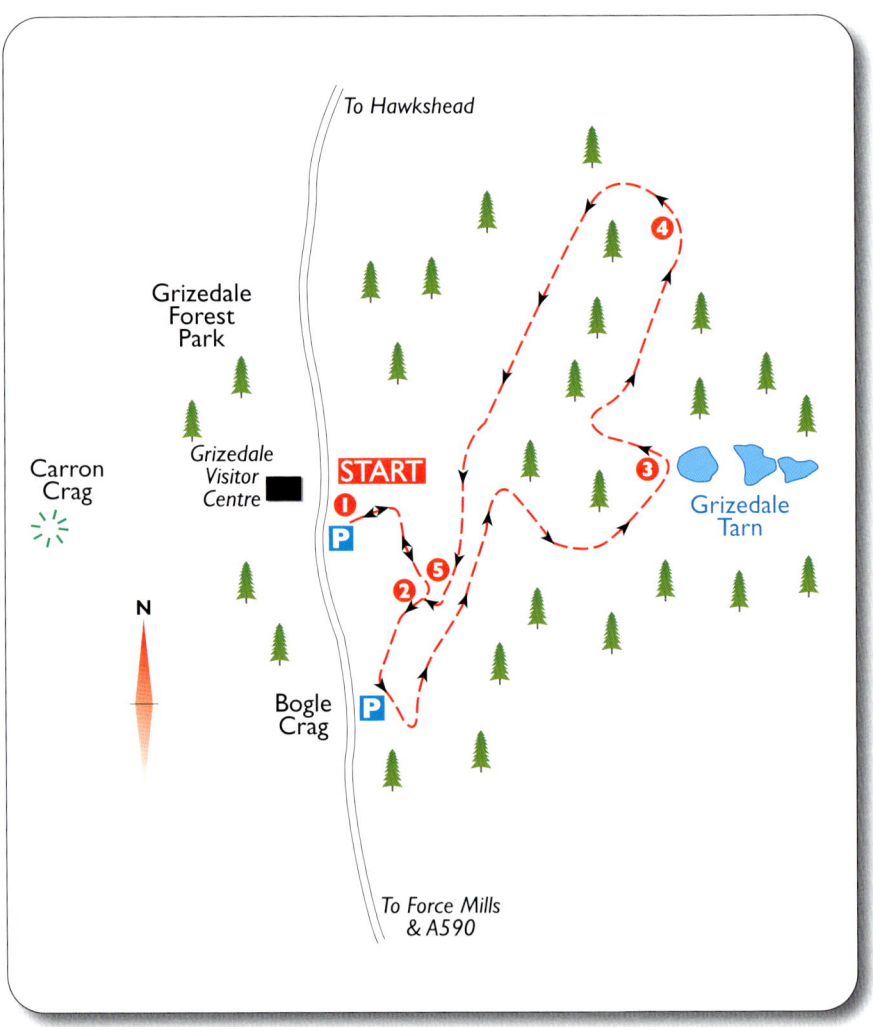

Grizedale Tarn

The Walk

1 In the car park, where you'll find a toilet block with water bowls for dogs outside, head to the place where all the forest trails start. You'll be following the **Grizedale Tarn** route which is marked with white wooden posts. The first part of the walk instantly takes you through a piece of forest sculpture in the form of the **Larch Arch**, and then following the concrete path is easy.

2 Before long you arrive at a shelter and soon after you head across a bridge, turning right when you reach the other side of the valley. The **white markers** are dotted along this track as you head straight on, but soon they will guide you up the hill to the left, and you follow a steep section of the path. This takes you up the hill, turning to the left at the top and over a small stream. Ignore a path that goes off to the right and keep heading straight on, down into a little dip and up the other side after crossing a stream. For a while it looks as though you're about to leave the forest, but the route branches round to the right and takes you back into the trees. Follow the track further up the hill, with a stream running down on your right. Again following the **white markers**, you turn right onto another track and then turn right again when you are brought out onto a larger forestry track. Follow the route round a sharp turn to the left to a statue of a **giant fox** on the left. Keep looking for the **white markers** and you'll see that the walk turns off and makes for another track on the right. This is a substantial track that meanders through the forest, giving you plenty of opportunity to enjoy the wealth of mosses, lichen, ferns, pine trees and silver birch that give this forest a special feel. You start to head downhill, with the track bending to the left and passing some large rocks.

3 Keep your eyes open for a **white marker** on the left which shows you the point at which you turn off and head through a section of the forest that brings you out at **Grizedale Tarn**. Once you've spent some time there, look for the path that brings you back out at the original track you were on, again following the markers, and go straight ahead when you reach the crossroads. You'll soon be turning off to the right on a track and heading downhill quite steeply on a path that doubles up as a river during heavy rain.

4 Keep heading down, using stepping stones to cross over a small stream before continuing your descent. You'll bend round to the left as you carry on walking downhill. Eventually you end up walking down a series of steps and are brought out at a larger track, where you turn left. Look out for a path down on the right that is signalled by a **white marker** and take this; you'll be able to see two other white markers straight away here, so you'll know you're on the right track. Continue walking downhill, curving to the right and heading

The Lake District – A Dog Walker's Guide

over a stream. At a junction of paths turn right, following the signs for the **visitor centre**. When you come to a fork in the path, take the route on the left and stick with the white markers once more.

5 Cross over a wooden footbridge and stick to the path as it bends round to the right and underneath the bridge that you went over at the start of the walk. Continue ahead on the path and you'll find that it doubles back on itself and takes you to the upper bridge. Instead of crossing it this time, head straight on and pass the shelter before marching through the **Larch Arch** and back to the car park.

These deer won't be scared by dogs!

Elterwater

A view of the Langdale Pikes across Elter Water

A very popular there-and-back walk that has everything dog owners need. There is space away from roads for your canine to run around, plenty of chances for a swim and a dog-friendly café at the halfway point to enjoy cake and a pot of tea.

Great Langdale is one of the most famous valleys in England, let alone the Lake District. Its beauty and grandeur has attracted and smitten tourists and artists for centuries. Although Great Langdale is the official name for this huge, sweeping glacial valley, many shorten it to 'Langdale', but the full title is needed to distinguish it from nearby Little Langdale. Elterwater, where this walk starts, is one of only two villages in Great Langdale, the sparse population adding to its remote, rugged charm. Today, the main industry supporting the local economy in Elterwater is tourism. In the past there were thriving

The Lake District – A Dog Walker's Guide

quarrying and agricultural industries, and, going back even further into the past, important Neolithic activity. Archaeologists have found the remains of Neolithic axes all over Britain and have traced many of them back to Langdale after analysing the rock and minerals used in the polished axes. Greenstone is made up of fine-grained material that can be traced to the Langdale slopes around Harrison Stickle and Pike O' Stickle. Those making the axes could have quarried the stone from these mountain areas, or the rocks could simply have been collected from the ground by scree slopes. The village of Elterwater shares its name with the nearby lake, although the latter's name is split into two words, Elter Water. It actually lies half a mile or so to the south-east of the village, along this very easy-to-follow route. The lake is 930 m long and, at the widest point, is 320 m across. The deepest part of Elter Water falls to a depth of 15 m and, while it may seem a peaceful and tranquil setting, it would certainly not be a great idea to take a boat out on it; the outflow of the River Brathay is very strong and leads to a fierce waterfall. As for the name Elter Water, it can be translated as 'the lake inhabited by the swans' and swans are still winter residents here.

Terrain
Care must be taken around Skelwith Force, but the main track from Elterwater to Skelwith Bridge is easy-going and poses few problems.

Where to park
There is a National Trust pay and display car park in the centre of Elterwater village (GR NY328047). **Map:** OS Explorer OL7 The English Lakes: South-eastern area.

How to get there
Unless you are coming over the mountains along the Wrynose Pass, it's best to approach Elterwater from the east. Head for Skelwith Bridge on the A593 between Ambleside and Coniston. Once there, you'll see the signs off the main road for Elterwater.

Dog factors
Distance: 2.7 miles.
Road walking: No roads, but look out for traffic as you approach the car park at Chesters.
Livestock: None.
Stiles: None.
Nearest vets: Oak Hill Vet Group, 1 Church Street, Ambleside.

Elterwater 13

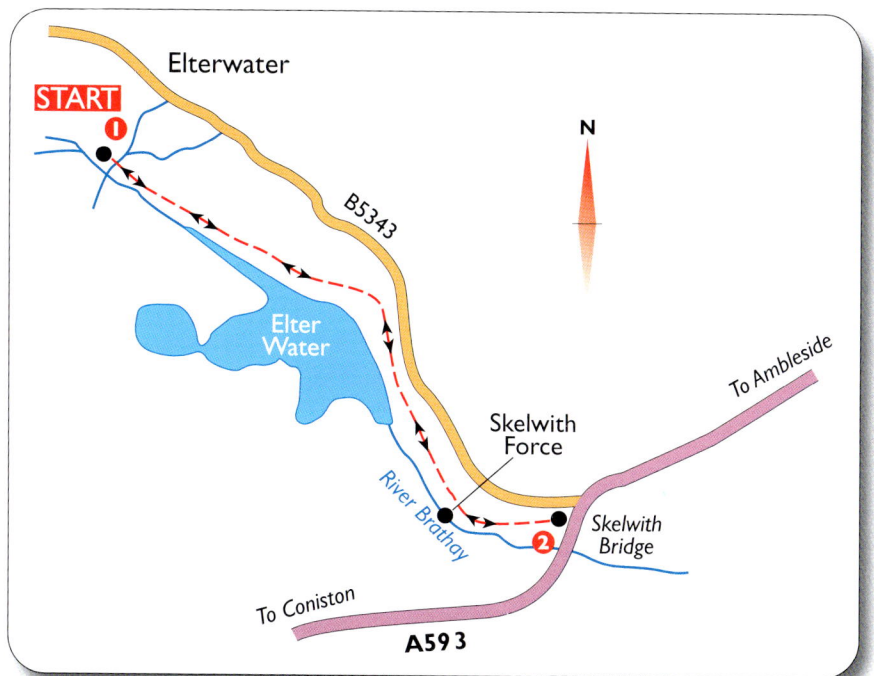

Nearest refreshments

There are places to eat and drink at both ends of this walk. Try the Britannia Inn at Elterwater ☎ 01539 437210, www.thebritanniainn.com, LA22 9HP and, a little further away at Chapel Stile, Wainright's Inn, which is ever-popular with walkers. ☎ 01539 438088, LA22 9JD. Halfway along the walk at Skelwith Bridge, Chesters is a great place where you will find a hall of fame for dogs who have had their picture taken next to the shop's sign. ☎ 01539 434711 www.chestersbytheriver.co.uk LA22 9NJ

The Walk

❶ From the National Trust car park head towards the river and turn left onto the path that runs by the side of it. Go through the gate and walk by the slate wall on the right, with the river flowing steadily beyond it and fields stretching out on your left. The path soon becomes a very level and carefully laid slate route, with off-lead time from the outset and plenty of doggy attractions. Go over a wooden bridge as a stream enters the larger river. The path becomes

The Lake District – A Dog Walker's Guide

a little more rocky as it leaves the river for a while and enters a wooded section. You will soon come across **Elter Water** on the right, a stretch of water that provides plenty of chances for your dog to play, explore and exercise. The path continues along the length of Elter Water before thinning out and forming a river. Before this happens, keep an eye out on the river bank for the small 'Danger' sign that warns of the impending waterfall of **Skelwith Force** for any boats straying this far. Sticking to the path, press onwards and go through a gate. Follow the path straight on, keeping the river on your right, until you come out at **Skelwith Bridge**, where you'll find **Chesters**, a popular place to buy food and drink.

❷ Having refreshed yourself, it's a case of retracing your footsteps back up the valley to the Elterwater car park. First be sure to venture down the steps to see the waterfalls at close hand, being careful all the while as the **River Brathay** is fast-flowing and the rocks can be slippery.

Calmer water is a good chance for a drink.

Tarn Hows

Tarn Hows is a popular beauty spot with artists and photographers.

This idyllic location is in the hands of the National Trust and makes a perfect circular dog walk. As well as off-lead time and plenty of opportunities to play 'fetch' in the water, there are amazing views and a guaranteed charm no matter what the season. Tarn Hows is a must for the Lake District dog-walker and your pet will have plenty of chances to meet and greet other dogs along the way.

Tarn Hows is one of the most popular beauty spots in the Lake District, partly because of the accessibility of the walk. However, I have visited many times and in different seasons, and have never found that the number of visitors hampers a day out or detracts from the scenery. It is, quite simply, one of our country's gems. But here's the interesting thing; even though this is one of the most photographed and talked about of the Lake District scenes, it's not a natural landscape. The area once contained three small tarns, known

The Lake District – A Dog Walker's Guide

a little unimaginatively as Low Tarn, Middle Tarn and High Tarn, and served by a series of streams and mires that drained into them. Much of the land around the tarns was used for common grazing by locals until 1862, when an Enclosure Act meant that it fell into the portfolio of former Leeds MP, James Marshall. Once he had ownership he set about improving the appearance of the landscape, firstly extending the plantations of spruce, pine and larch which surround the water. Marshall then built the dam at Low Tarn which raised the water level to give us the larger expanse of water that we see today. So, like the rest of the Lake District, Tarn Hows has been changed by human hands and it is perhaps ironic that something which would be controversial today – the building of a dam – has helped to create one of the most popular landscapes in the National Park. Marshall died in 1873 and the land was left to his family, who eventually sold it in the 1930s to a certain Beatrix Potter. She then passed it on to the National Trust. Among other things, the Trust has moved the car park to make it less intrusive and built a toilet block facility. You'll also often find a National Trust member of staff on hand to offer advice, information and membership. Tarn Hows has been a Site of Special Scientific Interest for several decades.

Terrain
The well-used path has some relatively small slopes and good access.

Where to park
There is a clearly signed National Trust pay and display car park at Tarn Hows (GR SD326996). **Map:** OS Explorer OL7 The English Lakes: South-eastern area.

How to get there
Heading from Coniston on the A593, take the B5282 towards Hawkshead and then follow the signs for Tarn Hows. If you're coming from the north or east, leave Ambleside on the A593 for Coniston and before long you'll see the B5286 signed to the left for Hawkshead. Take this and again look out for the local signs to Tarn Hows.

Dog factors
Distance: 2 miles.
Road walking: One road to cross.
Livestock: None.
Stiles: None.
Nearest vets: Oak Hill Vet Group, 1 Church Street, Ambleside.

Tarn Hows 14

Nearest refreshments

It's worth visiting Hawkshead after the walk for a drink and a bite to eat. You'll find plenty of outlets ready to provide refreshments, including the Kings Arms Hotel in The Square. ☎ 01539 436372, www.kingsarmshawkshead.co.uk LA22 0NZ. Dogs are also welcome in the bar area at the Queen's Head on Main Street. ☎ 01539 436271, www.queensheadhawkshead.co.uk LA22 0NS.

The Walk

1 Leave the National Trust car park and cross the road to pick up a path at the other side. At the fork, bear left downhill. Continue down, taking in the wonderful views of the tarn on the right, until you reach a bridge. Go straight on, through a gate. You are now on the perimeter path that goes around the edge of the Tarn, always keeping the water on your right. Before long you'll come across one of several unusual dead trees that people have hammered coins into. Some of them are completely covered and it makes for an interesting sight, like a piece of rural sculpture. The hill up to the left is known as **Tom Heights**. As you stick to the path around the water's edge you'll come to a path junction with a signpost and here you need to go straight ahead, following the signs for **Hawks Head**, around the tarn.

2 The path then bends round to the right, continues through woodland and eventually emerges from it, going over a bridge where there is a seat and an ideal place to rest and enjoy a picnic. Keep on the perimeter path, following the signpost for **Coniston** and **Yew Dale** at the next junction. The views of the surrounding fells from this relatively quiet and hidden-away tarn are phenomenal, and you'll be

Mountain views at Tarn Hows.

The Lake District – A Dog Walker's Guide

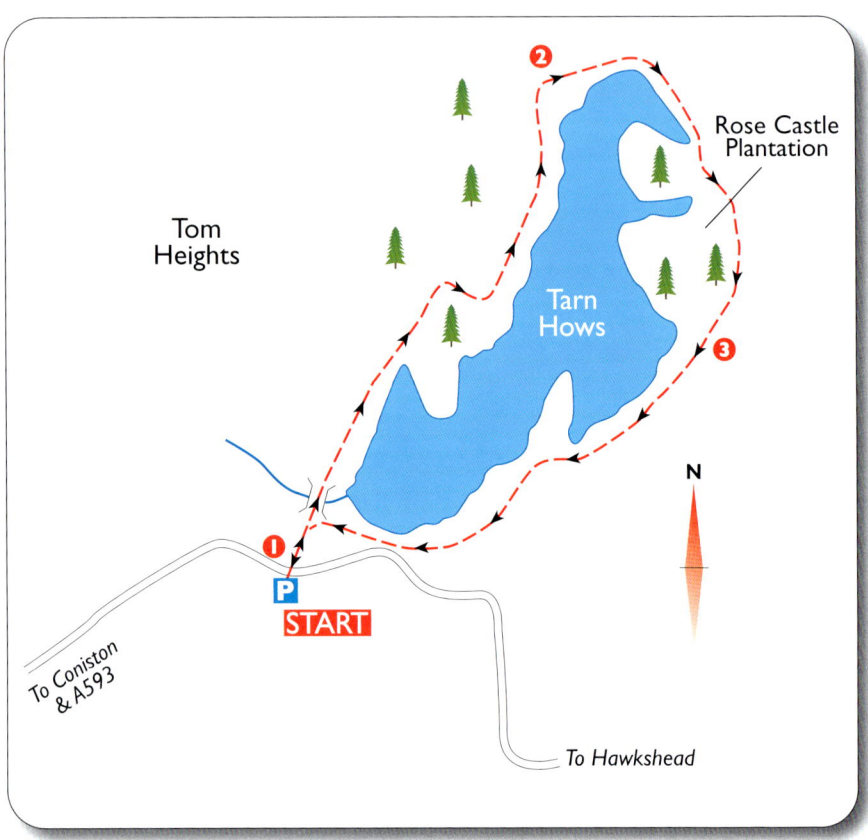

able to enjoy the sight of the Old Man of Coniston from one of several seats dotted around the route. Heading through another gate, there is a short section of uphill walking to complete before the route becomes more level. For a time you leave the side of the tarn, but before long you re-join it and can see the place from where you started the walk ahead to the right.

❸ As you approach the final stretch of the Tarn Hows circuit you will come to a fork in the path. Bear right, keeping close to the edge of the tarn. As with many sections of the walk, here is a great opportunity to take your dog down to the water and let it have a swim. The combination of tarn and many areas of woodland to explore, is why dog-owners come back to Tarn Hows time and time again. When you reach the bridge where you started out on the perimeter route, turn left and head up to the road. Carefully cross over, back to the car park.

15

Tilberthwaite

Magnificent views along the way.

A delightful circular stroll passing old slate industry sites, with off-lead time close to trees and a river. There are some idyllic views of Little Langdale on this walk, in a less-visited corner of the Lakes. Drystone walls and fences give dogs a chance to explore without their owners worrying.

The Lake District in numbers:
48,000: People living within the National Park boundary.
22,930: Homes in the National Park.
157: The number of cm Windermere rose after heavy rain in 2009.

The Lake District – A Dog Walker's Guide

Dog factors

Distance: 3 miles.
Road walking: The walk starts and ends with a short section of road walking on a very quiet country lane.
Livestock: There are places for off-lead time, but you are also likely to come across sheep in some fields and should use caution and attach the lead if unsure.
Stiles: None.
Nearest vets: Oak Hill Vet Group, 1 Church Street, Ambleside.

885: Square Miles covered by the Park.
1760: Listed buildings in the Lake District.
978: Metres above sea level at the highest point (Scafell Pike)
15: The percentage of dwellings that are second homes.
14,800,000: Tourists visiting the Lake District every year.
214: Fell tops identified by Alfred Wainwright.
89: People out of 100 travel to the Lake District by car.
74: The depth of Wastwater in metres.
2061: Average rainfall in mm.

Terrain

These are good tracks to follow, with some steep slopes.

Where to park

The National Trust car park in Tilberthwaite. (GR NY306010). **Maps:** OS Explorer OL7 The English Lakes, South-eastern area, and OS Explorer OL6 The English Lakes: South-western area.

How to get there

Just north of Coniston village on the A593 is a turning off towards High Tilberthwaite. Head along it almost as far as High Tilberthwaite, which is at the end of the small country road, and you'll find the car park on the left.

Nearest refreshments

There are no refreshments to be had on this remote Lake District walk, so best head into Coniston when you've finished. In the centre you'll find the Black Bull, with its award-winning micro-brewery on Coppermines Road. Tel: 01539 441335 www.blackbullconiston.co.uk LA21 8DU. A little off the beaten track on a road heading up the hill, on Sun Hill to be precise, is the Sun Inn, which is another pub welcoming friendly dogs. Tel: 01539 441248, LA21 8QH.

Tilberthwaite 15

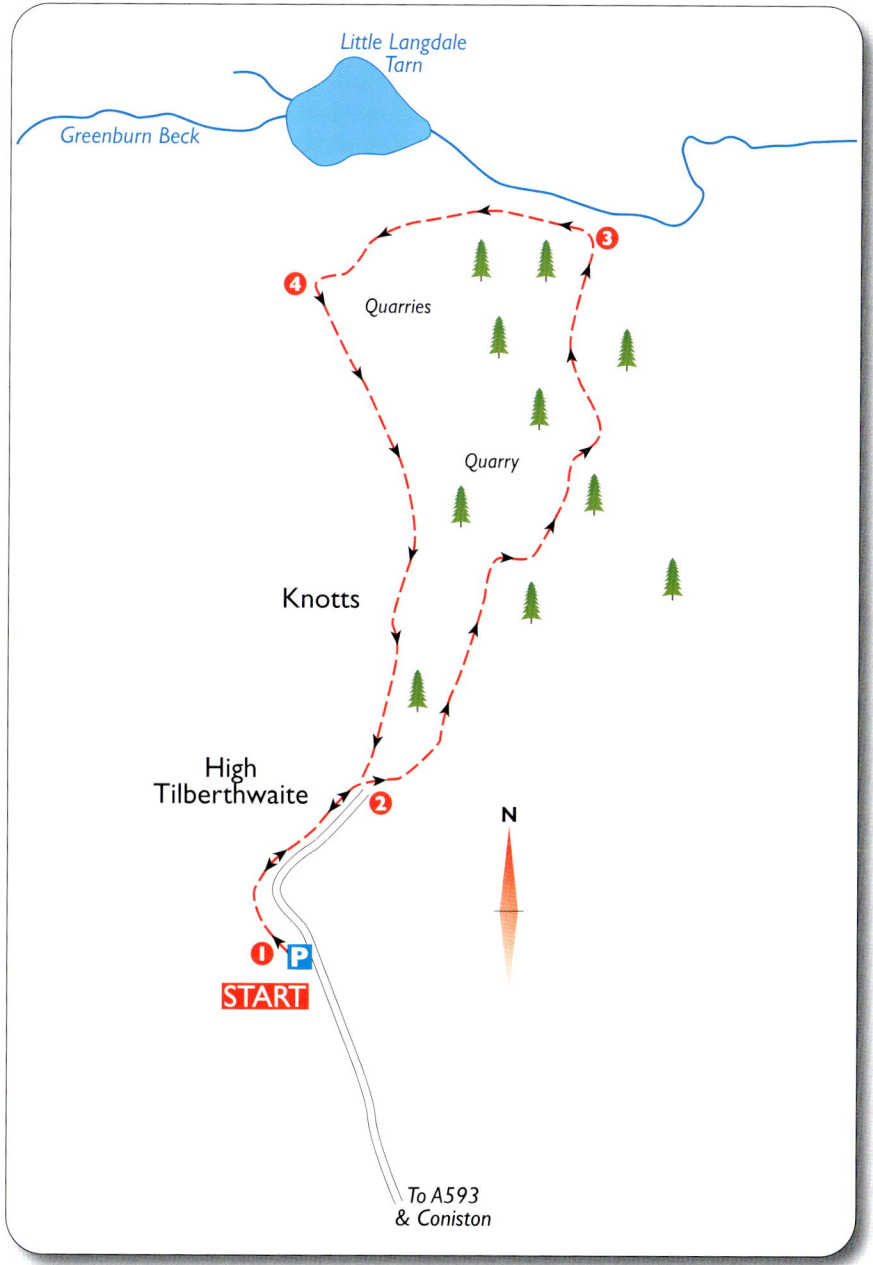

The Lake District – A Dog Walker's Guide

The Walk

① From the National Trust car park head to the road and turn left. You leave behind the signs of an old quarry around the car park, but you're going to be passing much more evidence of this industry which supported local people in days gone by and still provides a living for those working in the few quarries operating today.

② Continue along the road to a farm where you'll find a choice of two tracks when you go beyond the buildings. Bear right, onto the bridleway; you'll be returning by the other track once the circular part of the walk is complete. There are plenty of opportunities on this walk to let your dog off lead to explore the woods and river, but this is not one of them. You're likely to come across sheep in this field so keep your pet under control here, and keep an eye out for sheep. Continue straight ahead on the path and through a gate. Here you will become aware of the huge piles of slate that have been left here, like man-made scree slopes, a remnant of industrial times when the land employed more people in quarrying. Eventually, you will be walking on top of an old embankment. You now enter a wonderful area of woodland, following the track as it bends round to the left. Once again you pass a pile of slate on the left, in an area that is fine for dogs to be let off the lead to explore the trees. This section of the walk is enclosed by drystone walls and fences, meaning that dogs will be able to roam free, so long as you take a common sense approach. Still with walls on either side, you enter a darker section of the wood and approach a gate and the end of the path.

③ Do not cross the bridge, instead turn left on to a cycle track. Continue on this track, with the water on your right. You soon go through a gate and can see a picturesque bridge away to your right. This bridge would take you off towards Little Langdale, but we're not heading over that way on this walk so keep going straight ahead beyond it. You will now be able to see the magnificent valley of Little Langdale stretching ahead of you on the right, with Little Langdale Tarn in the valley bottom, below peaks such as Holling Crag, Horse Crags, Lingmoor Fell and Wrynose Fell.

④ Pass a building and follow the path as it turns off to the left, heading up a steep hill at first. Continue as the path bends round to the right, over a stream and through a gate. At a signpost and junction of paths, turn left and venture off towards **Tilberthwaite**, a mile away. Your dog will need a lead for this section as there are sheep about. Continue on, through a gate and over the fells, passing over rocks and enjoying great views of the surrounding countryside on

Tilberthwaite

this last part of the journey. Head on through another gate, then, bending round to the right soon, you can see large scree slopes of slate to the left. The path drops down, back to the farm. Head through a gate and turn right on the road to retrace your steps to the car park.

Bluebells in the woods in spring.

Rydal Water

A peaceful spot by Rydal Water.

Through woods and around an idyllic lake with fells rising on all sides; this walk rightly attracts many dog walkers and sends them home with a warm glow inside. An essential stroll and a perfect opportunity for your pet to socialise with other dogs.

Rydal Water is one of the smallest of Cumbria's principal lakes and sited near a quiet settlement of the same name, but don't let the size of the water or the local population fool you – this is a big hitter when it comes to quality walks. Rydal Water is actually a holding area for the River Rothay which flows through Grasmere and heads down into Windermere. There are no boats allowed on the water, except those authorised by Rydal Hall, meaning this stunning lake is always peaceful. There are also plenty of things to do in the local area, with Wordsworth's homes, Dove Cottage and Rydal Mount nearby.

Rydal Water 16

Dog factors

Distance: 2.6 miles.
Road walking: The route crosses a main road twice. There are two short sections along this road, and a short climb up a steep street.
Livestock: Mixed, use caution when entering areas with sheep.
Stiles: None.
Nearest vets: Oak Hill Vet Group, 1 Church Street, Ambleside.

Terrain
Good access, with some rocky sections and a short climb.

Where to park
The White Moss car park between Rydal and Grasmere (GR NY350065). **Map:** OS Explorer OL7 The English Lakes: South-eastern area.

How to get there
The car park is on the main road between Grasmere and Rydal. Take Junction 36 from the M6 and head for Windermere, then Ambleside. From here you will be able to pick up signs for Grasmere.

Nearest refreshments
You walk past the Badger Bar (Point 5) which is well worth a visit. ☎ 01539 434500 LA22 9LR www.theglenrothay.co.uk. For something a bit different, try the Apple Pie Café in nearby Ambleside, where dogs are welcome at all times. ☎ 01539 433679 LA22 9AN www.applepieambleside.co.uk

The Walk

1 From the White Moss car park head for the road and you'll see a gap in the wall opposite. Cross carefully and pick up the path at the other side. Follow this track through the trees, picking up a bigger track and turning right onto it through a picnic area.

2 At a footbridge on the left climb the steps and cross the river linking Grasmere with Rydal Water. At the other side enter **White Moss Wood** and follow the sign for the **Rydal Water path** which is easy to follow, flat at first but then climbing a little.

The Lake District – A Dog Walker's Guide

❸ The path winds up the small hill to a gate. Go through it and turn left down the track. Follow a drystone wall on the left, beyond which is **Rydal Water** with great views of the fells rising up at the other side. This is a popular place for walking the dog, and I'm sure your pet will be in good company on the route. The path eventually drops down to the edge of the water, which is ideal for dogs wanting a dip. Although the majority of the path is easy access, there is a large rocky section around the lake that you will need to climb carefully. Cross a stream over a footbridge. Here, be sure not to miss the views behind you as they are the finest from this route. Continue on the track and climb up towards another gate, heading away from the water.

❹ Through the gate there is a concrete track to follow, taking you by a farm on the right and towards a row of cottages. Opposite these dwellings take a footpath off to the left, down some steps and into the woods. At the bottom of this section, go through a kissing gate and out into an open field. Turn right and head for a footbridge over the **River Rothay**. Climb up the path at the other side to the A591. Turn right and walk on the path next to the road.

❺ You pass the **Badger Bar** at this point, which could well be a good place to take a rest. The route goes beyond it, and turns left up the first road, opposite Rydal Lodge. Climb up the road, which is a very steep section of the walk.

❻ Go past **Rydal Hall** on the right and keep on beyond **Rydal Mount** on the left. Just after this, turn left on a path signed for Grasmere, along an old coffin route. After starting level and even, the path becomes more uneven after passing through the first gate, then dips down, giving good views of Rydal

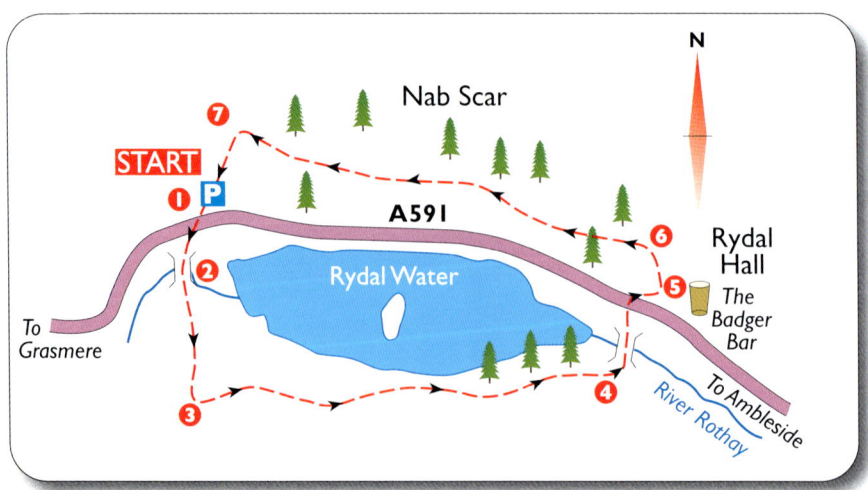

Rydal Water 16

Water on the left. Follow this track through gates and over streams, until you eventually come to a great viewpoint with a couple of benches where you can sit and take it all in. Over more streams and then through another gate, there are a few rocky climbs to negotiate on this section.

7 After another gate look out for an unsigned path down to the left. It's a substantial track, next to a house on the right, that leads steeply down by a river and eventually to the main road. Turn right when you reach the road, keeping on the path, and you'll see the car park in front of you.

Plenty for your dog to explore.

Sizergh

Stunning medieval Sizergh Castle.

One of the National Trust's great Lake District properties, there's plenty to see and do at Sizergh for all the family. This walk takes you on a peaceful route past the castle. There are woods for your dog to explore, while you can stop and admire the stunning views.

Unlike many of the splendid National Trust properties, Sizergh Castle doesn't just look back on an aristocratic history, for this is still very much a family home. As such, it's not possible to look around the castle every day of the week. Check opening times because on occasions the rooms and the gardens are closed to the public to give the Strickland family some privacy. The land crossed by this route was once owned by the Deincourt family, but passed to the Strickland family when Elizabeth Deincourt married Sir William de Stirkeland in 1239. The Stricklands held the castle for centuries until it was gifted to the National Trust in 1950. The castle and surrounding land falls into the Parish of Helsington, which also incorporates nearby Brigsteer and has a population of just under 300. Dogs are welcome on the estate at Sizergh, but not in the garden.

Sizergh 17

Dog factors
Distance: 2.8 miles.
Road walking: None.
Livestock: Likely to meet some en route. Common sense approach needed.
Stiles: None.
Nearest vets: Westmorland Veterinary Group, Riverside Business Park, Kendal.

Terrain
Some inclines, but not too steep. All well-signed tracks.

Where to park
Parking is available at the National Trust car park at Helsington church (GR SD488889). **Map:** OS Explorer OL7 The English Lakes: South-eastern area.

How to get there
From the M6 at Junction 36, follow signs to Kendal and then pick up the route to Sizergh Castle, which is well indicated via brown tourist signs. Before you reach Sizergh Castle, take the turning off towards Brigsteer on the right. As you enter Brigsteer, follow a signed track to the left towards the National Trust car park and viewpoint.

Nearest refreshments
The Strickland Arms at Sizergh is a popular dog-friendly pub. ☎ 01539 561010, LA8 8DZ, www.thestricklandarms.com. Another option is the Punchbowl Inn at Crosthwaite. ☎ 01539 568237, LA8 8HR www.the-punchbowl.co.uk. There is a picnic area and café at Sizergh Castle.

The Walk

1 As you face the church from the parking area, follow the main path to the right, basically continuing in the direction you were driving in. Straight away you're treated to amazing views of the valley, the fell range off to the right and Morecambe Bay to the left. You'll have a drystone wall on the left as you head down the track and through a gate.

The Lake District – A Dog Walker's Guide

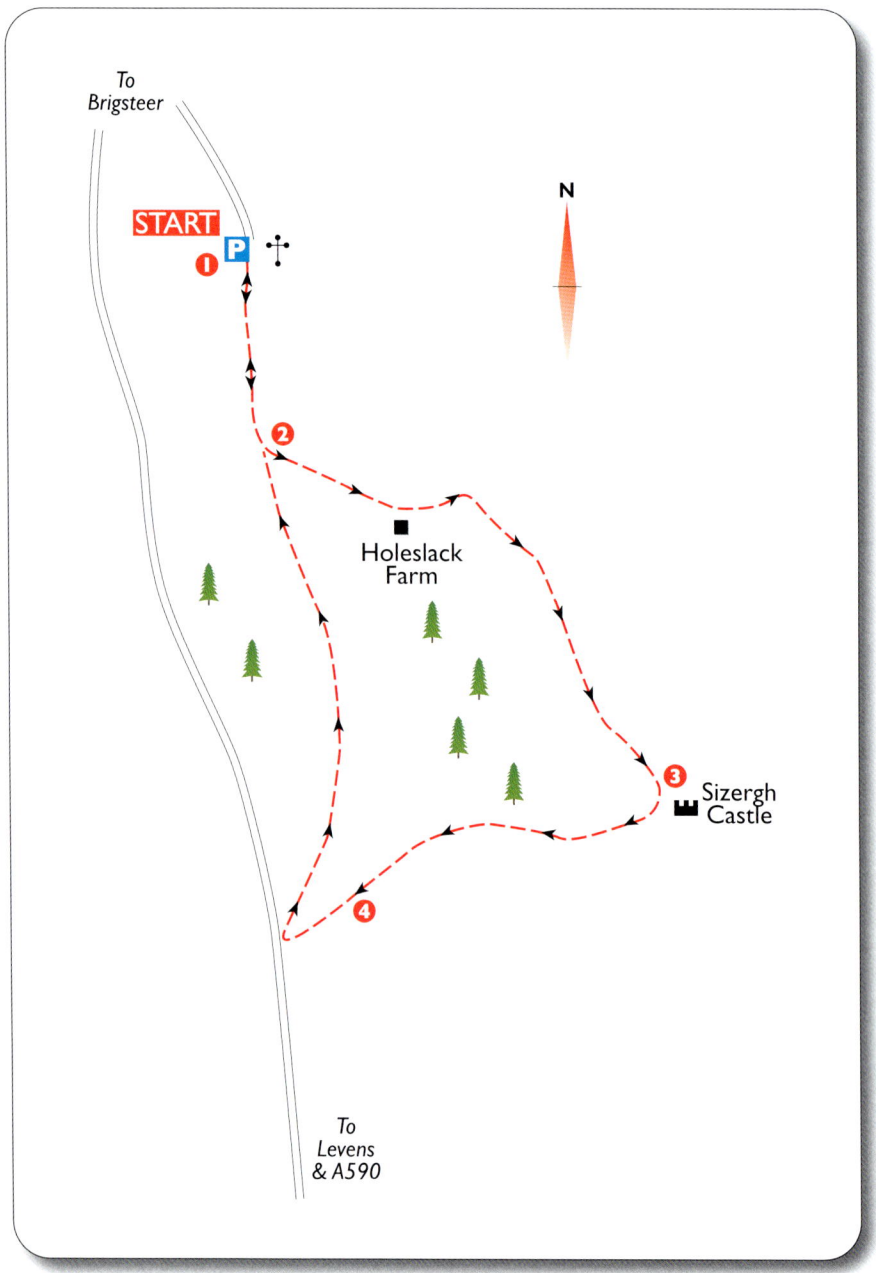

Sizergh

2 Bear left on a concrete track that starts to go down, leading you to the National Trust holiday cottages at **Holeslack Farm**. Go through a gate and head straight across on the track, eventually going through another gate and down the hill. As you continue down, you pass an old farm building and go through another gate, all the time sticking to a very straight-forward path that will eventually bring you out at **Sizergh Castle**. There is a dog bin here. Pass through the gate to the picnic area and café.

3 When you've finished exploring here, head back beyond the gate you came through and follow the path to **Brigsteer Wood**. After a couple of gates the path reaches more open fields.

4 Continue straight ahead to a country road. Don't go onto the road, but take the new path that doubles back a little on the right. This takes you winding up the grassy hill, passing woods on the right. Follow markers and the grassy track to the top and you'll reach a gate which leads you out onto a track through the woods. You come out onto a field, with great views of the fells off to the left that include Coniston Old Man and Harrison Stickle. The next gate you reach brings you to a track. Turn left and you're on your way back to where the walk started.

Woods and fields to explore.

Wray Castle

Stopping to feed the swans.

This is a delightful walk along the western shore of Windermere with woods, streams and, of course, the lake to explore. It will keep even the most inquisitive dog busy for a long time, and there's a castle to admire at the halfway point.

Wray Castle has been through many phases of ownership and been used for several different purposes down the decades. What was once a holiday home for Beatrix Potter's family, has also been used as a training college for the Merchant Navy and as a family home. It was donated to the National Trust in 1929. Until a few years ago, the plan had been to turn Wray Castle into a high quality hotel. Everything was in place for the work to be carried out, but then financial problems meant that the National Trust decided to open it to the public instead. When you stand outside the front doors on the driveway admiring the view across the lake, you can clearly see why. The National Trust are in the process of restoring the grounds to how they would have looked when the house was built. Dogs are welcome in the grounds on leads.

Wray Castle

Dog factors

Distance: 2.7 miles.
Road walking: None.
Livestock: None.
Stiles: None.
Nearest vets: Oak Hill Vet Group, 1 Church Street, Ambleside.

Terrain
There is a fairly steep climb up to the castle itself, but the path by the lakeside is easy-going. Be aware that there are often cyclists by the lake.

Where to park
The National Trust's Red Nab car park is at the end of a long lane from High Wray. (GR SD385995). **Map:** OS Explorer OL7 The English Lakes: Southeastern area.

How to get there
Head towards High Wray village, close to the western shore of Windermere. At the centre of the village there is a turning off to the south. This road takes you straight to the Red Nab car park, which is as far as you can go on the road in a car. The track continues for walkers and cyclists down to the Windermere Ferry.

Nearest refreshments
The small village of Outgate, to the west of High Wray on the B5286, is home to the Outgate Inn, where dogs are welcomed. ☎ 015394 68329 www.outgateinn.co.uk LA22 0NQ. A little further north at Barngates, the Drunken Duck Inn is well known and they are happy for dogs to go in the bar. ☎ 015394 36347 www.drunkenduckinn.co.uk LA22 0NG.

The Walk

❶ Facing Windermere, take the path heading left from the car park towards Wray Castle. This is a there-and-back walk to give maximum off-lead time and the greatest pleasure by the side of the water, and can always be extended by continuing along the track when you've completed the walk shown on the map. This will take you on an easy route further south along the shore of Windermere. For the walk described here, take the path to the north, along

The Lake District – A Dog Walker's Guide

the shore of Windermere towards Wray Castle. You'll pass a bench, with trees on the right between you and the water, your dog all the time enjoying the investigative pleasures on offer. Across the lake to the far right you can make out the well-known horseshoe walk from Ambleside via Fairfield. Less strenuous than that classic ramble, our route goes on ahead. Watch out for cyclists as this is also a popular cycle path. Leaving the wooded area behind, fields will now open up on your left beyond a drystone wall. On a clear day you can see right across Windermere towards Ambleside and you may hear the wake of a fair few boats lapping on the shore next to you. Soon the path

Wray Castle 18

Lots to investigate.

bends round to the left and you enter **High Wray Bay**, which is a good place to let dogs off the lead and in the water.

② After passing through a gate follow the path towards Wray church. You pass a boat house on your right and proceed on through another gate, before turning right towards Wray Castle and entering the **Wray Castle Estate**. Take the path to the left and climb up the hill to Wray Castle, where there's the chance to have a rest on the benches outside.

③ Retrace your footsteps back to the car park by the lake at the **Red Nab**, but remember you can continue beyond there on the cycle path to extend your shore-side walk.

19

Kendal

The view from Hawes Bridge at the start of the walk.

As well as enjoying a countryside trail along what used to be the Lancaster Canal, you could take a detour to explore the ruins of Kendal Castle, a popular place for dog walkers and an atmospheric island of history in the east of the town. The towpath is a very popular spot with Kendal dog walkers so there are plenty of opportunities for your dog to socialize and play. The path is also fenced in places so you can walk without worrying about livestock.

Mention 'Kendal' and, for many, the words 'mint cake' will follow. Among casual walkers, serious hikers and tourists with no interest in exerting themselves, Kendal Mint Cake is well known as an energy-giving weapon in the adventurer's toolkit. The packet of Kendal Mint Cake you buy on your Lake District trip may go no further than Cumbria before it's devoured, but important packs have been to the extremes of the world, including on expeditions to Mount Everest, K2 and both poles. The origins of the sugary formula, according to legend, can be traced back to 1869 and are said to have

Kendal 19

been stumbled upon accidentally. Although different manufacturers have different claims, the common understanding is that Kendal confectioner Joseph Wiper was experimenting and searching for a clear glacier mint. He took his eye off the cooking pan for a bit too long and the cloudy result was his mint cake. Production began at his small Kendal factory and, in a stroke of marketing genius, the glucose-based piece of stamina-boosting confectionary was advertised as energy food.

Terrain
Following an old canal route for most of the journey, this walk is largely on the level, with some small inclines elsewhere.

Where to park
There is room for some roadside parking at Hawes Bridge. If these limited spaces are gone, you may have to park further along the road and walk to the starting point. **Map:** OS Explorer OL7 The English Lakes: South-eastern area.

How to get there
The starting point for the walk is a small country road between Natland and the A591. To reach this, take the A590 from Junction 36 of the M6 and then follow signs for Windermere on the A591. Shortly after joining the A591, take a turning off to the right for Prizet and Natland.

Nearest refreshments
Try out the Factory Tap on Aynam Road, which is dog friendly. ☎ 01539 482541, LA9 7DE www.thefactorytap.co.uk. The Oddfellows pub in Kendal has treats and drinks available for you and your dog. ☎ 01539 722459, LA9 4RL. The Riverside Bar and Hotel has a good range of drinks and meals, as well as dog-friendly rooms for overnight stays. ☎ 01539 734861 www.riversidekendal.co.uk LA9 6EL.

Dog factors
Distance: 4 miles.
Road walking: A very small section along a road and a couple of roads to cross over.
Livestock: Depending on the season, you may come across farm animals in the first and last sections of the walk.
Stiles: 2.
Nearest vets: Highgate Veterinary Clinic, 173 Highgate, Kendal.

The Lake District – A Dog Walker's Guide

The Walk

① The walk starts from **Hawes Bridge**, on the small country road between Prizet and Natland. Take a look over the bridge at the waterfall below and, while still looking towards Kendal, head to the right bank of the river.

② Go up the road and then take the footpath off to Kendal on the left. Straight away you enter a small section of woodland with the river on the left. This is an ideal place to let dogs explore and roam about amongst the trees after your car journey. Continue ahead on the path and look out for livestock as you pass through a thin gap to a field. Cross over the field and pass through a gate, heading over the next field before coming to a stile. Keeping the river close by on the left, you again have a narrow gap to squeeze through and another gate. You'll be able to see the fells of the Lake District appearing in the distance and when the river meanders off to the left, stick to the path straight ahead, keeping to the left of the grassy mound ahead of you. Turn right along the path and head to **Natland Road**.

③ Turn left along the road and then cross over to rejoin the trail by the former

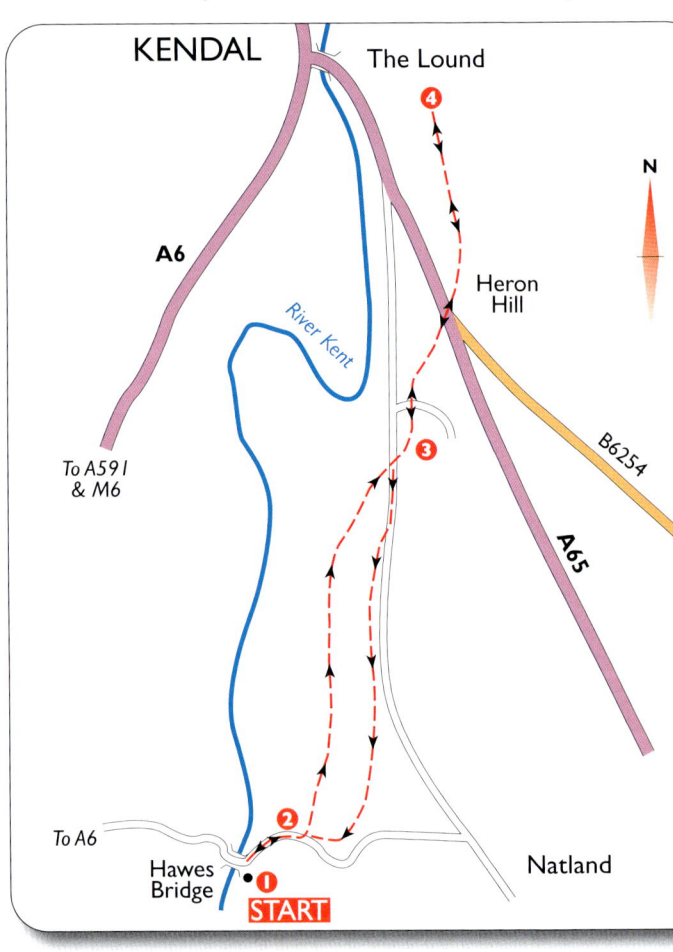

90

Kendal 19

Lancaster Canal towards Kendal. This is a large section of off-lead time where you are bound to see other like-minded dog owners giving their pet the chance to stretch their legs. Simply stick to the well-established trail as it heads beneath an old canal bridge. Put your dog on a lead as you come to the **A65**, where you'll see a crossing ahead of you that will help you get to the other side to pick up the canal trail once again. Continue the walk into Kendal, following signs for Canal Head North, a mile away. The path bends round to the left and you'll soon see a school sports ground on the right. Continue ahead under the historic canal bridge number 186 and before long you will come to **Park Side Road**.

❹ If you want to explore Kendal town centre and the castle at this point, follow the signs left for the central area, which isn't too far away but make sure you keep a note of where you are because you will need to return to this path to complete the walk. Alternatively, turn around and begin walking back down the canal route. Pass under bridge number 186 and continue, again taking advantage of the off-lead time. Cross the road and continue on the **Lancaster Canal Trust trail** at the other side, following the sign for **Tewitfield**. Go under another bridge then straight on for a while along the road. Soon after, cross over and turn left. Follow the canal path again when you see it signed off to the right. The first part of this trail is the old towpath. It is fenced in and your dog can roam around freely. The walk enters a series of fields, including a couple of stiles between them, before coming across a truly bizarre sight – an old bridge that once crossed the old canal, but now spans nothing more than a field as the canal has been filled in. The old towpath is still there, however, making this one of the most interesting human additions to the Cumbrian countryside. Shortly after the bridge, walk along the top of an embankment built for the canal. Go through a gate at the end of the field onto a country road. Turn right and head downhill to get back to your starting point.

A short detour takes you to the ruins of Kendal Castle.

Eskdale

Admiring the view across the valley.

This is a great way to discover this tremendous valley, from the fells down to the coast. You can either walk the full length of the Eskdale Trail and combine it with a ride on the historic steam railway, or treat it as a there and back walk from Dalegarth, choosing a length to suit you. There's plenty of off-lead time on this walk, with trees, ferns and streams to discover. Any inquisitive dog is sure to have a blast and run off plenty of energy.

When you start this walk close to the Cumbrian coast, you are likely to see the steam trains that chug up and down Eskdale between Ravenglass and Dalegarth near Boot. Even listening to the 'toot' of the engines can brighten up your day and transport you back in time. The railway, of course, was not built for the tourist trade. This narrow-gauge line dates back to 1875 when

Eskdale 20

iron ore was mined around Boot and then carried down to the main line at Ravenglass, so industrial reasons were behind its development. But passengers were allowed to travel on the trains from 1876 until 1908; soon after this, in 1913, the line was closed due to a fall in demand for iron ore and dwindling passenger numbers. Two model makers bought and converted the line, starting passenger services and transporting granite. The line was sold once again in 1960, this time to the Ravenglass and Eskdale Railway Preservation Society. Today, this is a very popular attraction in the Lake District, operating 16 trains a day on peak days for about 120,000 passengers a year. Dogs are allowed on the steam trains at a cost of £1.50 per dog. For more information about times, check the website: www.ravenglass-railway.co.uk.

Terrain
Some steep climbs and rocky paths but you can rest and admire the view from the window of the steam train on the way back.

Where to park
Park at the pay and display car park at Dalegarth station (GR NY173007).
Map: OS Explorer OL6 The English Lakes: South-western area.

How to get there
From Junction 36 of the M6, follow signs for Barrow and take the A590. Turn off on the A595 towards Whitehaven and take the road up the coast to Ravenglass. Turn off the A595 just before crossing the River Esk and follow the signs for Eskdale Green and Dalegarth.

Nearest refreshments
At the Ravenglass end try The Inn at Ravenglass on Main Street. ☎ 01229 717230, CA18 1SQ, www.facebook.com/innatravenglass. Near the station at Dalegarth, try the Brook House Inn at Boot. ☎ 01946 723288, CA19 1TG, www.brookhouseinn.co.uk

Dog factors
Distance: 8.5 miles.
Road walking: Short distances as part of the Eskdale Trail.
Livestock: The route is largely fenced off, but there is always the chance of encountering sheep so use caution.
Stiles: None.
Nearest vets: Browne and Mckinney, Church Street, Broughton-in-Furness.

The Lake District – A Dog Walker's Guide

The Walk

❶ The Eskdale Trail is a popular route for dog walkers and cyclists, but it has to be said that it is not the best signed path in the world, so I'd advise you to take an OS map and follow these instructions carefully. From **Dalegarth for Boot station**, head to the end of the platform towards the road and turn right onto it.

❷ Keep on down the road and take the first track off to the left opposite the old school house, signed towards the Stanley Force waterfall. Continue winding down and over a bridge. Stick to this track and head through a gate and then round to the left at the other side.

❸ After climbing for 50 m or so the path turns sharply off to the right onto level pasture, following a sign for the **Eskdale Trail**. This takes you through a field, passing a house on the right and through another gate into woodland over some rocky ground and through several gates. You'll see the river on your right and notice that the path gets narrower. Leave the woods, through a gate and across a field. With the river still to your right, pick up the track and continue straight ahead, through a couple more gates. When the path forks, keep to the right and soon come out at a road.

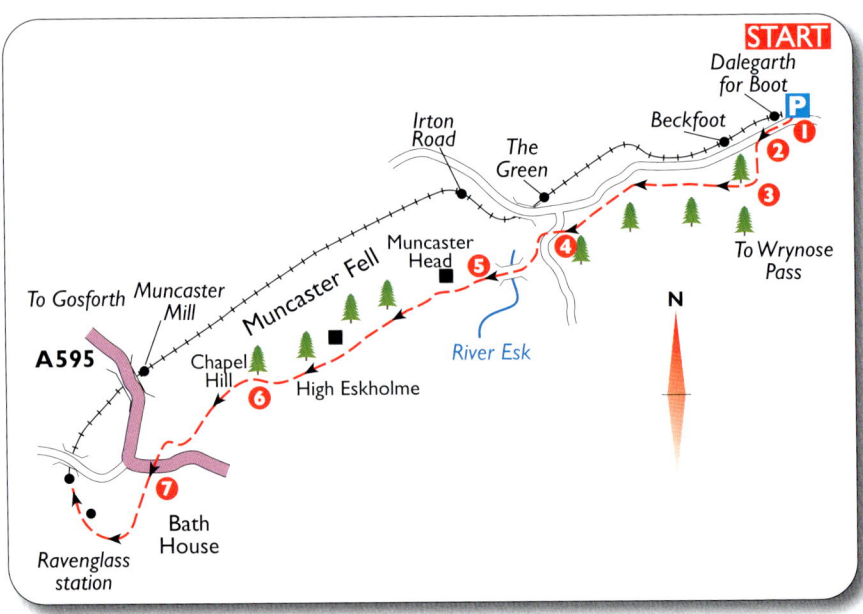

Eskdale

4 The route turns off to the left here, but the King George IV pub is about 400 m to the right if you fancy a diversion. After turning left at the road, watch out for a row of houses on the left as the road bends to the left. At this point take a track to the right signed for Muncaster Castle on the Eskdale Trail. With trees on either side, you head over a bridge and press on as farmland opens up all around you, and fells rise up in the distance.

5 This easy-going trail takes you beyond **Muncaster Head Farm** and begins to climb. Muncaster Head Farm is three miles into the walk and unless you are pressing on down to Ravenglass and using the train, you may decide to turn back here and make it a six mile there-and-back walk. If you are going the full distance to return on the steam train, the track continues winding its way through a wood. When you get to **High Eskholme**, continue beyond the house for around 250 m and then bear right off the tarmac lane and go up onto the forest track.

6 This is the toughest climb of the entire walk, heading up **Chapel Hill**. At the top you'll reach a well-established track and you need to turn left onto it, going downhill. This will bring you out at the main road, but don't go onto it, instead turn right onto a track, and then take a track on the left to cross the field.

7 At the main road once more, cross over carefully and head through the gateway towards the information centre. The Eskdale Trail to **Ravenglass** goes right from here, descending down through the woods. You'll come out at a road. Turn right onto it and follow it past the Roman Bath House on the right and continue beyond the campsite on the right. You'll come to a road; turn left onto it and go downhill to find the train station on the left after going under the bridge.

An iconic Lake District dry stone wall.

APPENDIX

Small Animal Veterinary Practices

The following are all vets that are close to the walks described. They have been selected as handling small animals and dogs in particular.

Browne and McKinney
East View, Church Street, Broughton-in-Furness LA20 6HJ.
☎ 01229 716230   www.browneandmckinney.co.uk

Frame, Swift and Partners
The Veterinary Centre, Carleton, Penrith CA11 8TZ. ☎ 01768 862454
www.frameswiftandpartners.co.uk

Highgate Veterinary Clinic
173 Highgate, Kendal LA9 4EN. ☎ 01539 721344
www.highgate-vets.co.uk

Millcroft Veterinary Group
Southey Hill, Keswick CA12 5NR. ☎ 0176 8772590
www.millcroftvets.co.uk

Millcroft Veterinary Group
Wakefield Road, Cockermouth CA13 0HR. ☎ 01900 826666
www.millcroftvets.co.uk

Oak Hill Vet Group
1 Church Street, Ambleside LA22 0BU. ☎ 015394 32631
www.oakhillvetgroup.co.uk

South Lakes Veterinary Centre
Victoria Road, Ulverston LA12 0BY. ☎ 01229 582900

West Lakeland Veterinary Group
55 Main Street, Egremont, CA22 2DB. ☎ 01946 820312
www.westlakelandvets.co.uk

Westmorland Veterinary Group
Riverside Business Park, Natland Road, Kendal, LA9 7SX. ☎ 01539 722692
www.westmorland-vets.co.uk